CW01302279

Copyright © 2021 by Tina Hom
Illustrations by various artists including
Tina Hom, Pencil Parker, and Annalise Art.

Fingerprint images designed by @pch.vector from Freepik.com

Published by MyGrateful.Life
Printed in the United States of America

All rights reserved. This copyrighted work may not be
duplicated, scanned or distributed in any form without permission.

ISBN 9798730077027

Hello!

This book belongs to:

WHAT IS GRATITUDE?

Gratitude is a feeling that focuses on noticing the good things happening in your life and being thankful for them.

WHAT IS MINDFULNESS?

Mindfulness means slowing down wherever you happen to be to focus your attention on whatever you are doing or seeing.

WHAT HAPPENS WHEN YOU PRACTICE GRATITUDE AND MINDFULNESS?

People have studied and found that when you practice gratitude and mindfulness regularly, you:

- ☆ Become a happier person
- ☆ Notice more positive things in your life
- ☆ Feel better about yourself
- ☆ Build better friendships and relationships with people
- ☆ Become stronger as a person inside and out
- ☆ Make better choices

WHAT CAN WE BE GRATEFUL FOR?

- ☆ Family and friends
- ☆ Teachers and health care workers
- ☆ A sunny or a snowy day
- ☆ Ice-cream, pizza or any of your favorite foods
- ☆ Really, anything!

HOW CAN WE BE MINDFUL?

- ☆ Take a few deep breaths in and out. Notice how it feels.
- ☆ Feel and describe different things indoors and outdoors.
- ☆ Do arts and crafts (paint, draw, color, make something...).
- ☆ Notice your surroundings. What do you see, hear, or smell?
- ☆ Eat something and pay attention to the flavors and textures.
- ☆ Notice how your feet and legs feel when you go for a walk.
    - Which part of your foot lands on the ground first?
    - Do you have a light or heavy step?
- ☆ Any activity where you pay attention to what you are doing.

INSTRUCTIONS

⚠️

THIS IS AN INTERACTIVE JOURNAL FOR KIDS.

THIS IS NOT YOUR TYPICAL GRATITUDE AND MINDFULNESS JOURNAL.

BE PREPARED TO DO SILLY THINGS, GET MESSY AND PUT STUFF IN YOUR JOURNAL THAT YOU'VE NEVER PUT IN OTHER JOURNALS.

#1 RULE :
HAVE FUN!

HOW TO USE THIS BOOK

①

YOU CAN GO IN ANY ORDER

②

PICTURES CAN BE COLORED

③

"EXTRAS" AT THE END OF THE BOOK ARE SO YOU CAN DO SOME OF THE ACTIVITIES AGAIN

④

BLANK NOTE PAGES AT THE END OF THIS BOOK CAN BE USED TO WRITE DOWN ANYTHING, EVEN PAGE NUMBERS SO YOU CAN GO BACK TO THOSE PAGES LATER

WHAT THREE THINGS ARE YOU THANKFUL FOR TODAY AND WHY?

FIND 2 OR 3 UNIQUE LEAVES OUTSIDE AND GLUE THEM TO THESE PAGES.

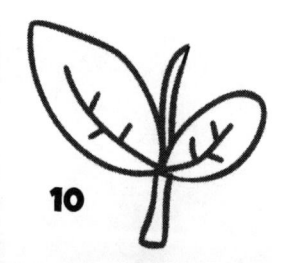

GIVE YOUR LEAVES NAMES AND EXPLAIN WHAT MAKES THEM SO SPECIAL.

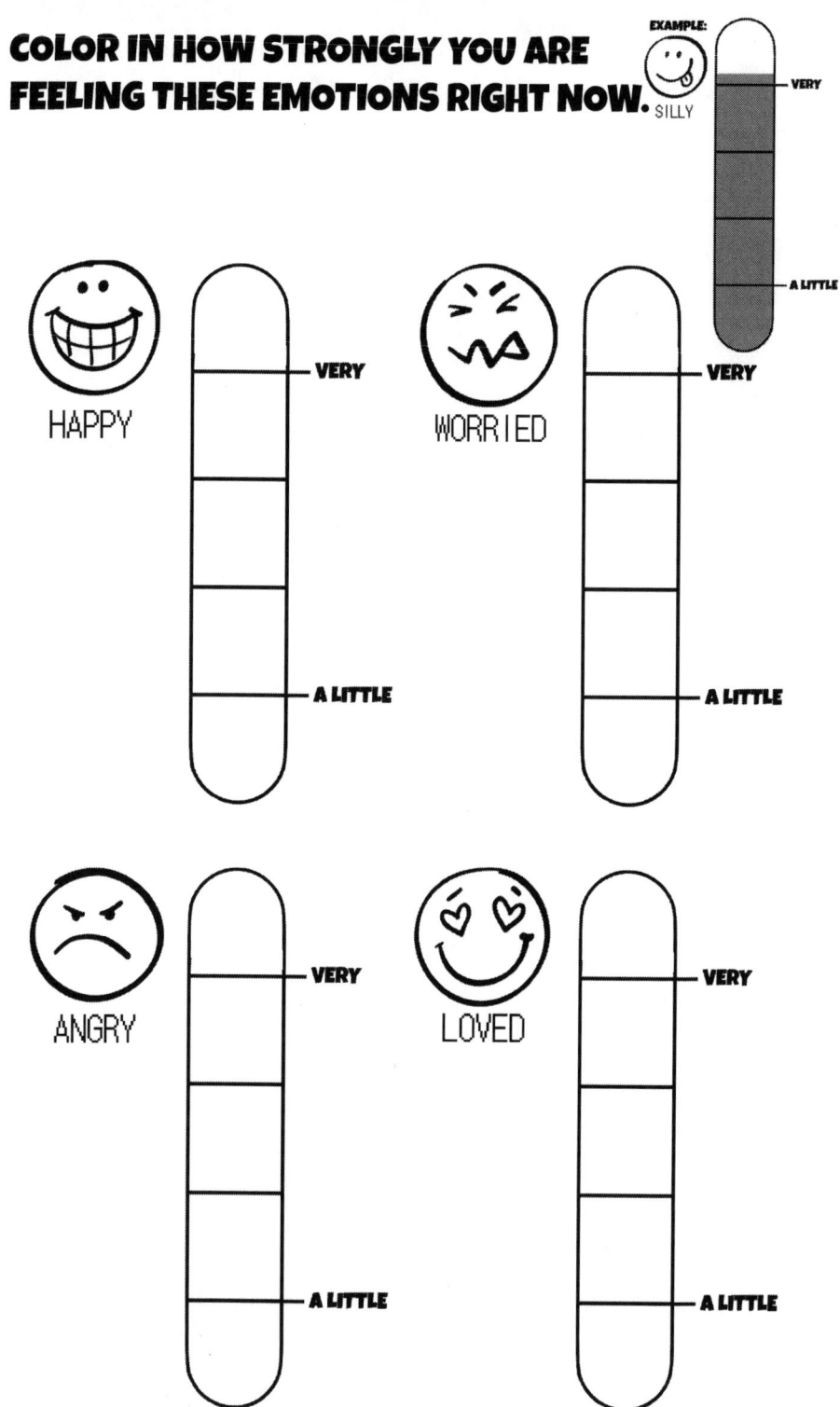

COLOR IN HOW STRONGLY YOU ARE FEELING THESE EMOTIONS RIGHT NOW.

EXAMPLE: SILLY — VERY / A LITTLE

HAPPY — VERY / A LITTLE

WORRIED — VERY / A LITTLE

ANGRY — VERY / A LITTLE

LOVED — VERY / A LITTLE

DESCRIBE HOW YOUR BODY FEELS WHEN YOU HAVE THESE EMOTIONS.

HAPPY

ANGRY

WORRIED

LOVED

HOW DOES YOUR BODY FEEL RIGHT NOW?

DRAW A PICTURE OF SOMEONE YOU ARE GRATEFUL FOR AND EXPLAIN WHY.

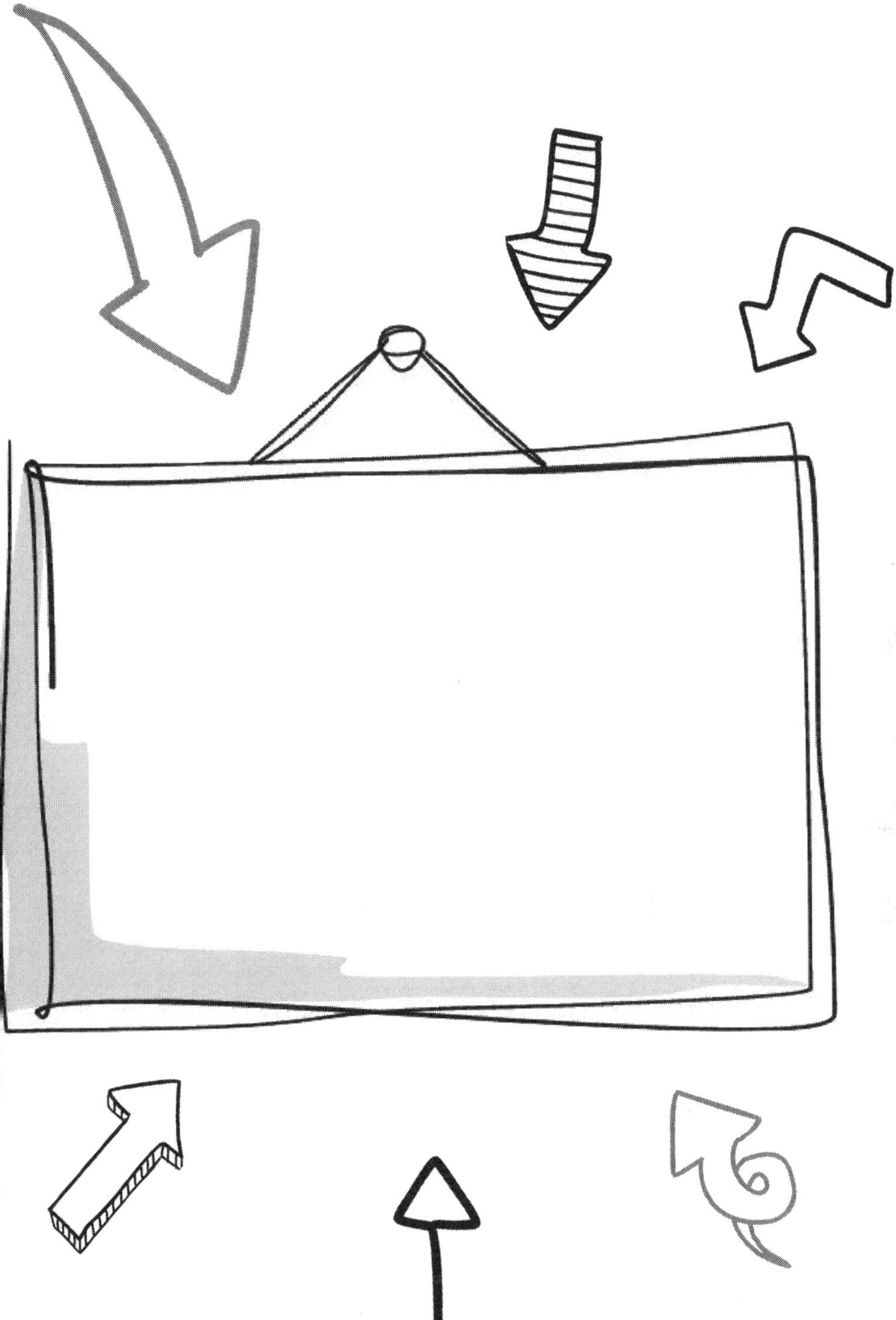

THINK OF YOUR FAVORITE COLOR. WRITE OR DRAW PICTURES OF THINGS THAT ARE THIS COLOR ON BOTH OF THESE PAGES.

DON'T FORGET TO COLOR THEM!

18 *EXTRA: A copy of this activity is at the back of this book.*

DRAW A PICTURE IN THIS BOX, THEN CAREFULLY TEAR OUT THE PAGE. CUT OUT THE PUZZLE ON THE BACK AND PIECE IT BACK TOGETHER AGAIN.

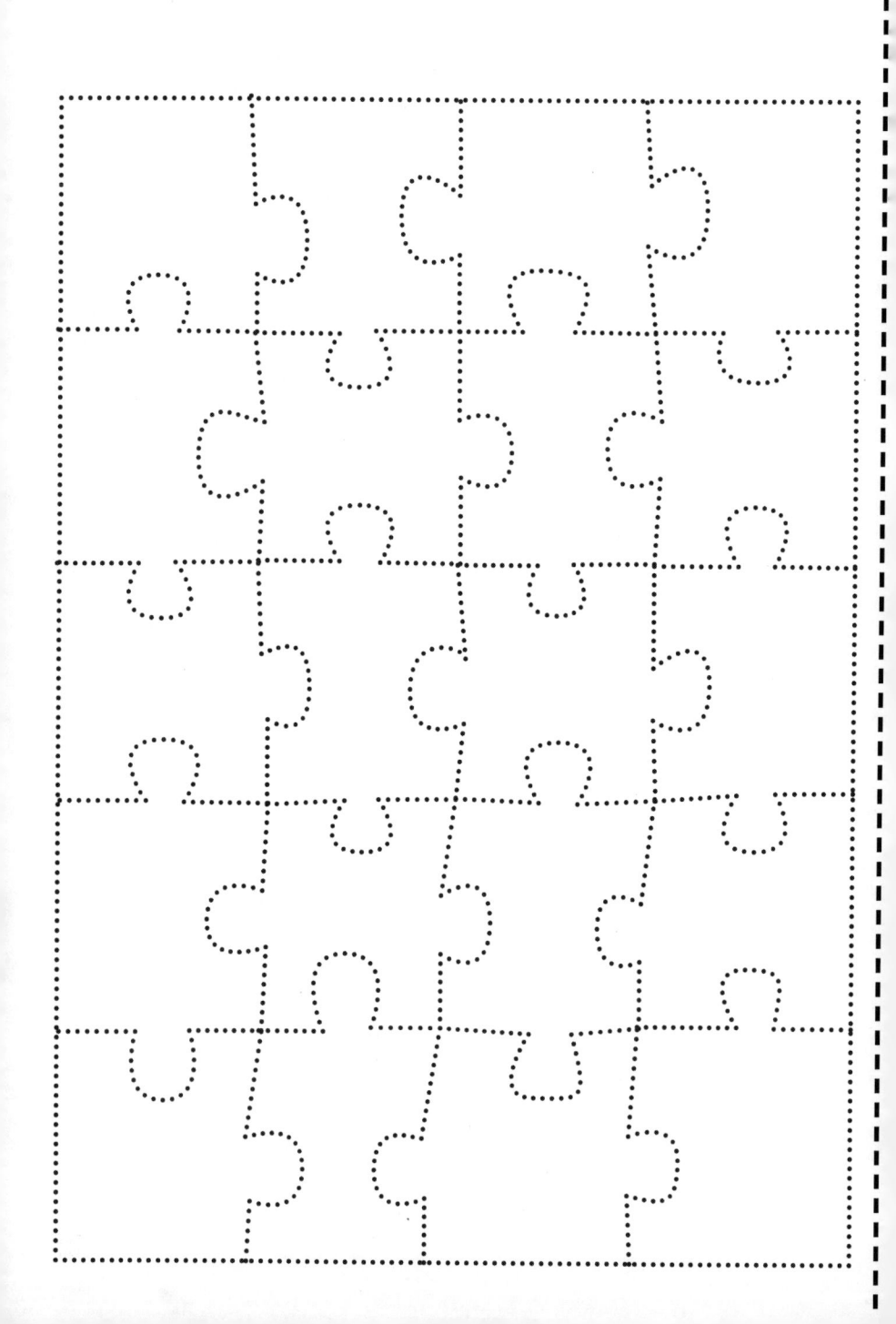

Cut out the puzzle on the dotted lines.

GRAB A PENCIL, CLOSE YOUR EYES AND DRAW A PICTURE OF YOURSELF.

DRAW YOUR FAVORITE SHAPE ALL OVER THESE TWO PAGES IN AN OVERLAPPING PATTERN.

COLOR THE SHAPES AND ENJOY YOUR WORK OF ART.

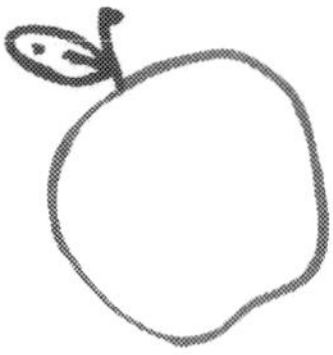
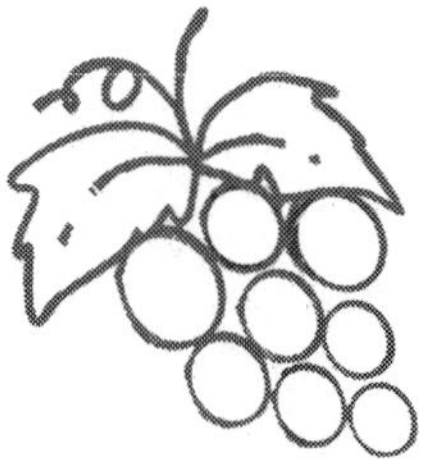
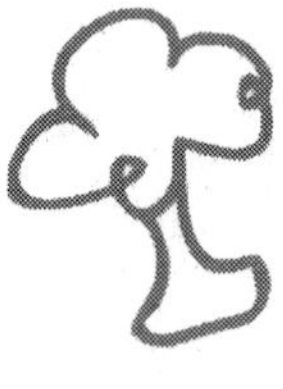
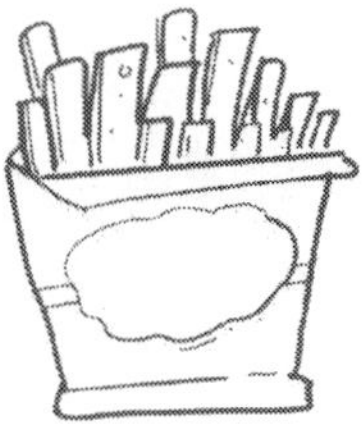
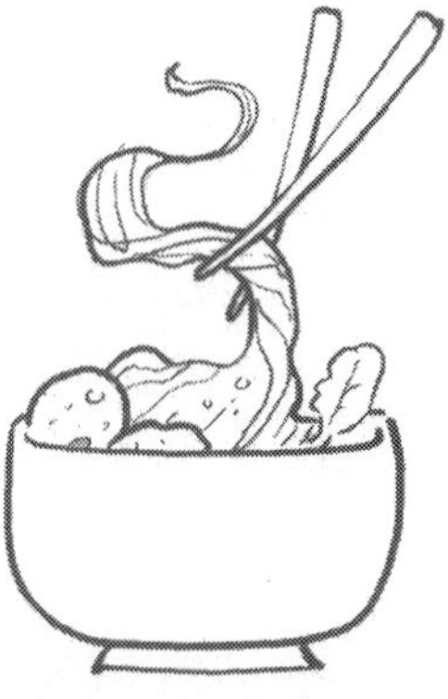
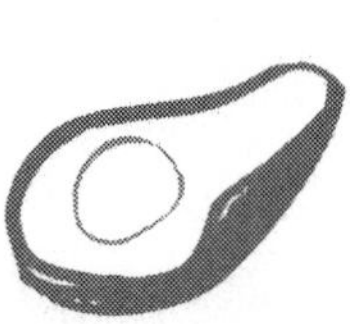

FIND SOMETHING YOU ENJOY EATING.
EAT IT AND ANSWER THE QUESTIONS BELOW.

1) This food was (circle one):

salty   sweet   sour   bitter

2) This food looked…

3) This food smelled…

4) This food feels _____ in my mouth.

5) I like eating this food because…

_____

_____

MAKE A COMIC STRIP ABOUT A GOOD DAY.

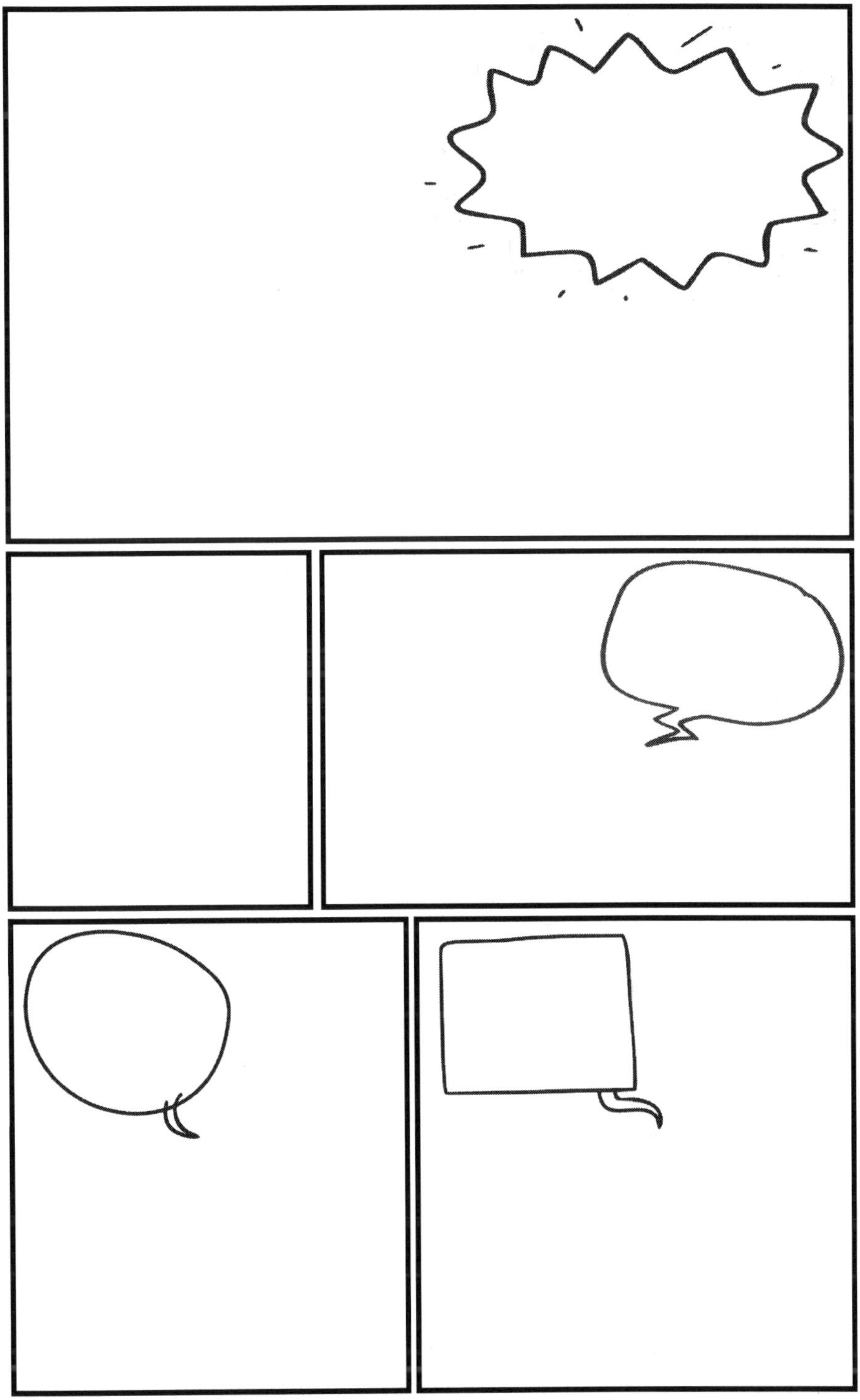

DRAW A SCRIBBLE IN THE BOX.

TURN THAT SCRIBBLE INTO A PICTURE OF SOMETHING.

NOW, IMAGINE A FUNNY STORY ABOUT YOUR SCRIBBLE AND WRITE ABOUT IT.

TRACE YOUR LEFT HAND ON THE LEFT PAGE.

WRITE DOWN OR DRAW THE THINGS OR PEOPLE YOU LOVE HAVING IN YOUR LIFE AND WANT TO HOLD ONTO IN YOUR LEFT HAND.

TRACE YOUR RIGHT HAND ON THE RIGHT PAGE.

WRITE DOWN OR DRAW THE THINGS THAT DON'T BRING YOU HAPPINESS THAT YOU WANT TO LET GO OF IN YOUR RIGHT HAND.

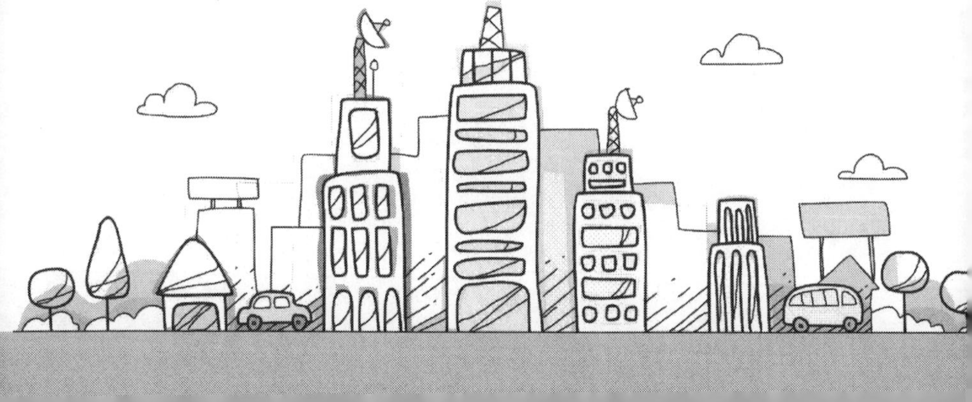

WRITE DOWN TEN REASONS YOU LOVE THE CITY YOU LIVE IN!

1)

2)

3)

4)

5)

6)

7)

8)

9)

10)

**WRITE A SECRET LETTER TO SOMEONE.
TELL THEM WHY YOU ARE THANKFUL FOR THEM.
GIVE AT LEAST THREE REASONS.**

IF YOU WANT, YOU CAN SECRETLY GIVE IT TO THEM.

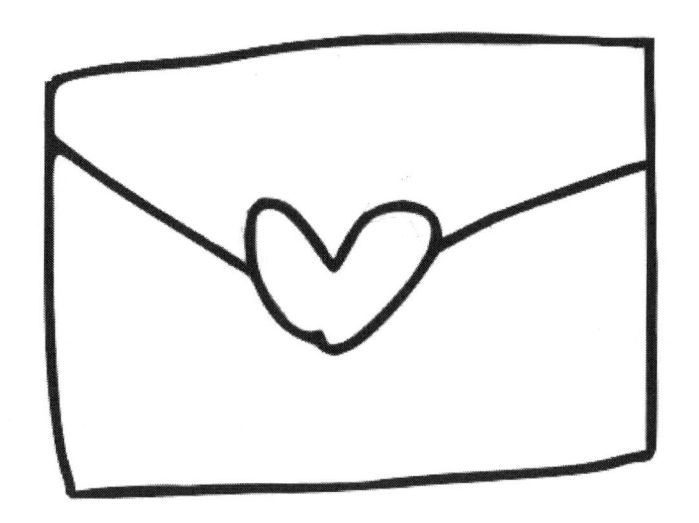

FILL YOUR BUCKET WITH THINGS PEOPLE CAN DO FOR YOU OR SAY TO YOU TO BRIGHTEN YOUR DAY?

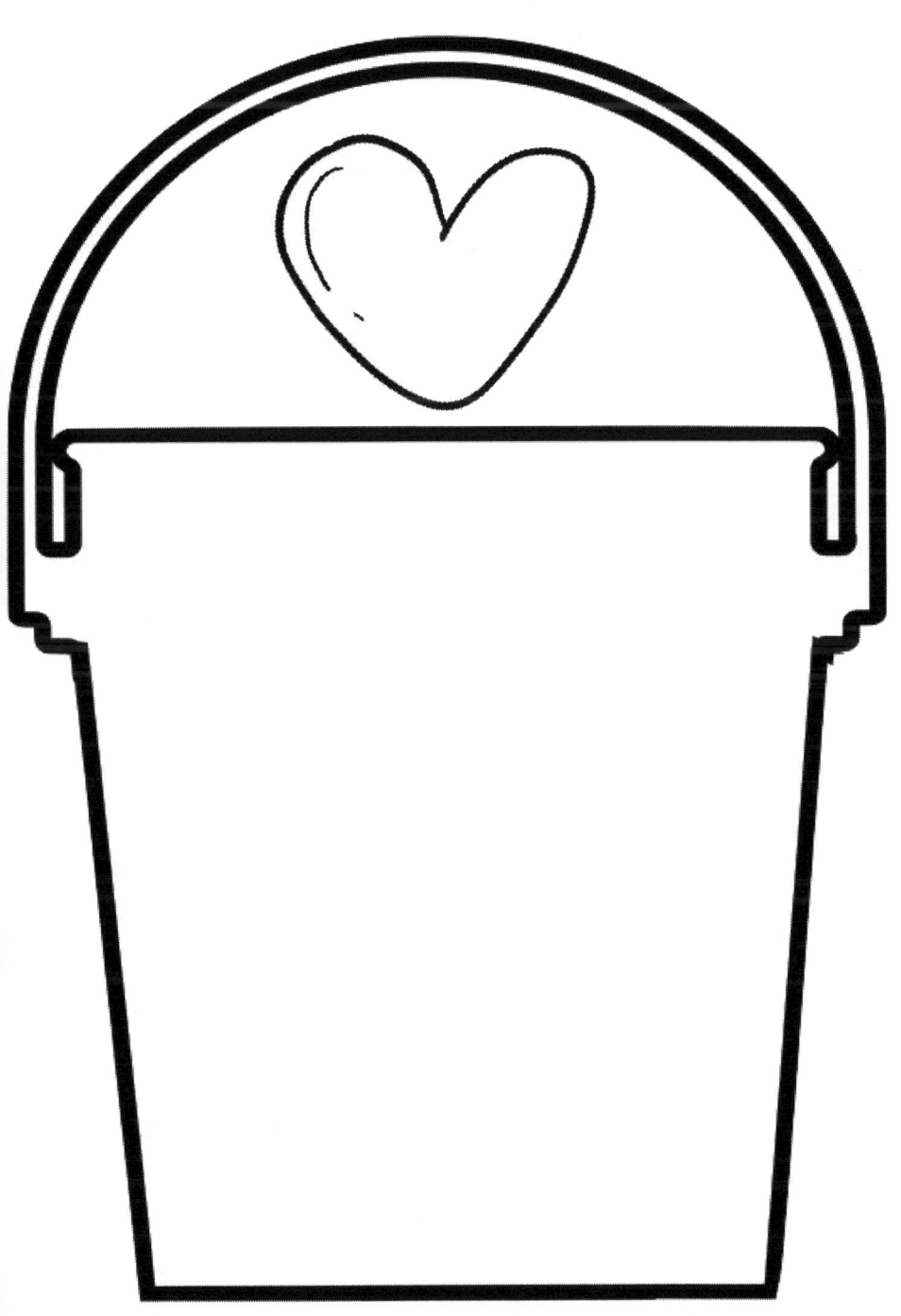

EXTRA: A copy of this activity is at the back of this book.

WHAT DO YOU THINK THESE LIVING THINGS ARE THANKFUL FOR?

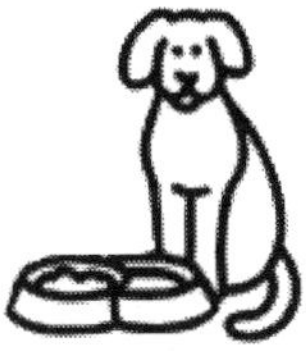

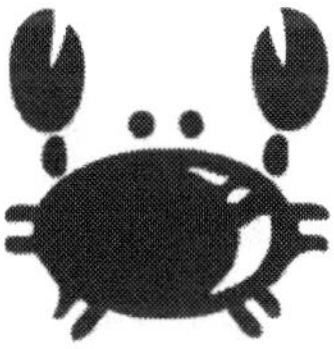

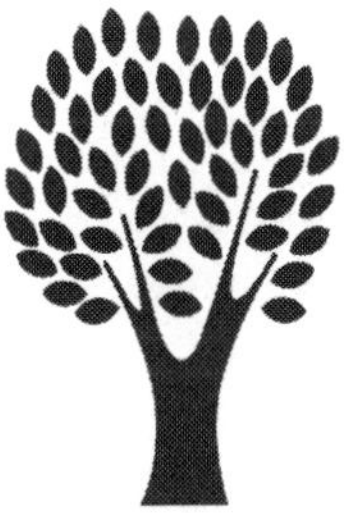

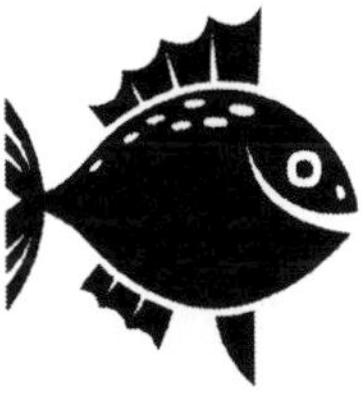

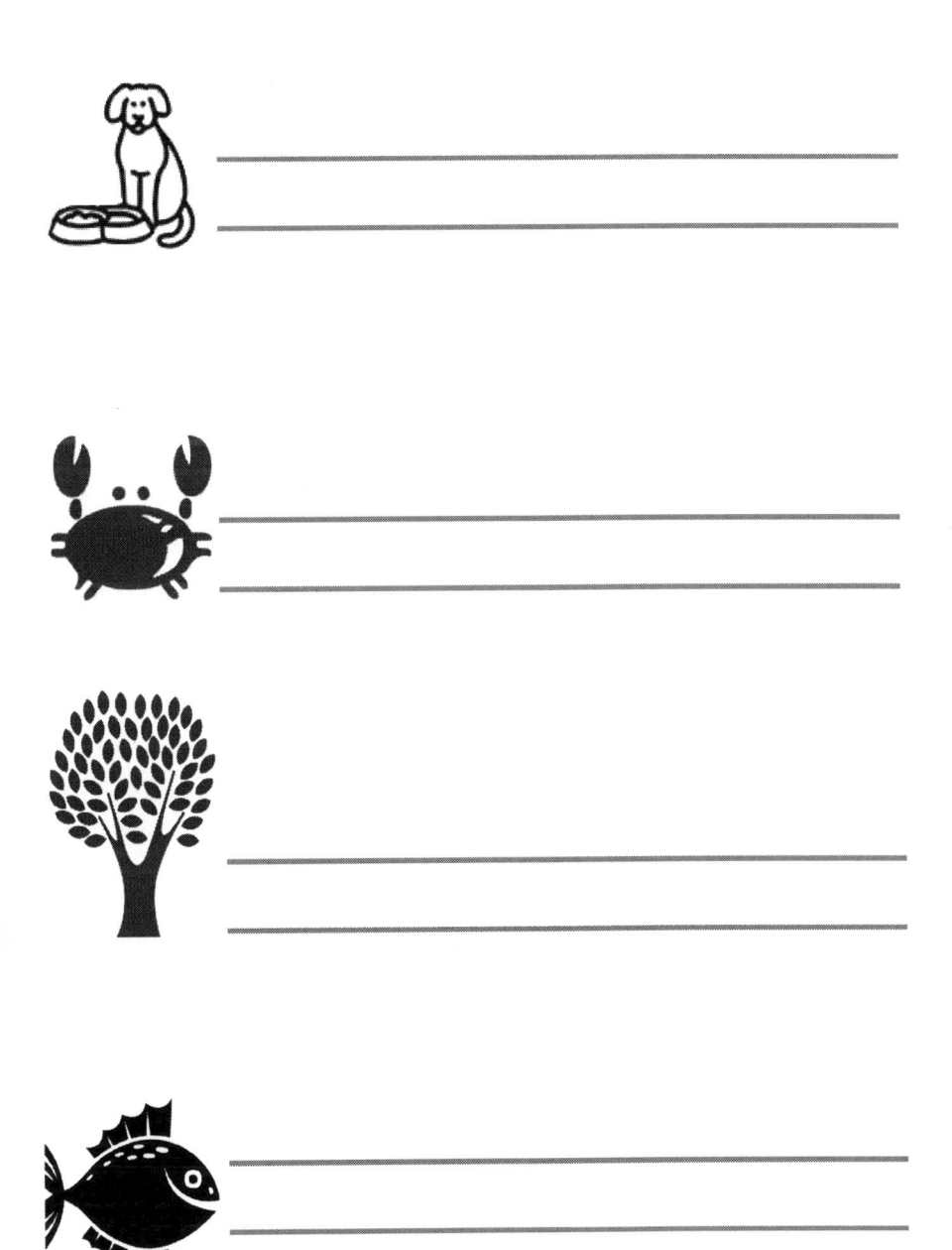

LET'S PRACTICE DEEP BREATHS

**PRETEND YOU'RE
SLOWLY SMELLING A FLOWER
THROUGH YOUR NOSE
UNTIL AIR FILLS YOUR BELLY.**

HOLD FOR 3 SECONDS.

USE THAT SAME BELLY AIR TO PRETEND YOU ARE SLOWLY BLOWING OUT BIRTHDAY CANDLES THROUGH YOUR MOUTH.

REPEAT THIS TWO MORE TIMES FROM THE BEGINNING.

COME BACK TO THIS PAGE TO PRACTICE DEEP BREATHS ANYTIME YOU FEEL WORRIED OR UPSET.

SIGN POSTS CHALLENGE

42 *EXTRA: A copy of this activity is at the back of this book.*

THINK OF AN OBJECT THAT YOU MIGHT SEE EVERDAY. EVERY TIME YOU SEE THIS OBJECT TODAY, WRITE DOWN SOMETHING YOU ARE GRATEFUL FOR.

OBJECT EXAMPLE: A BALL, A PAINTING, OR A PLANT...

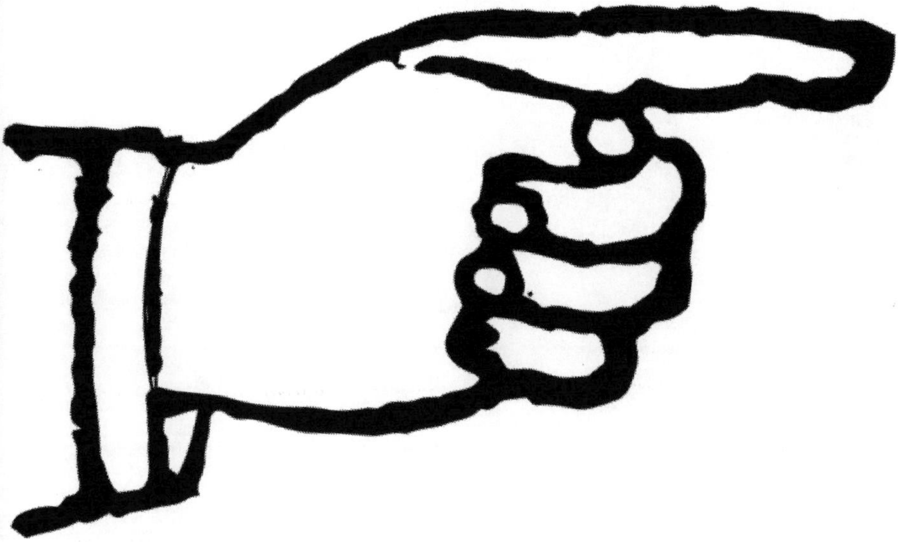

WRITE A THANK YOU NOTE TO YOURSELF.

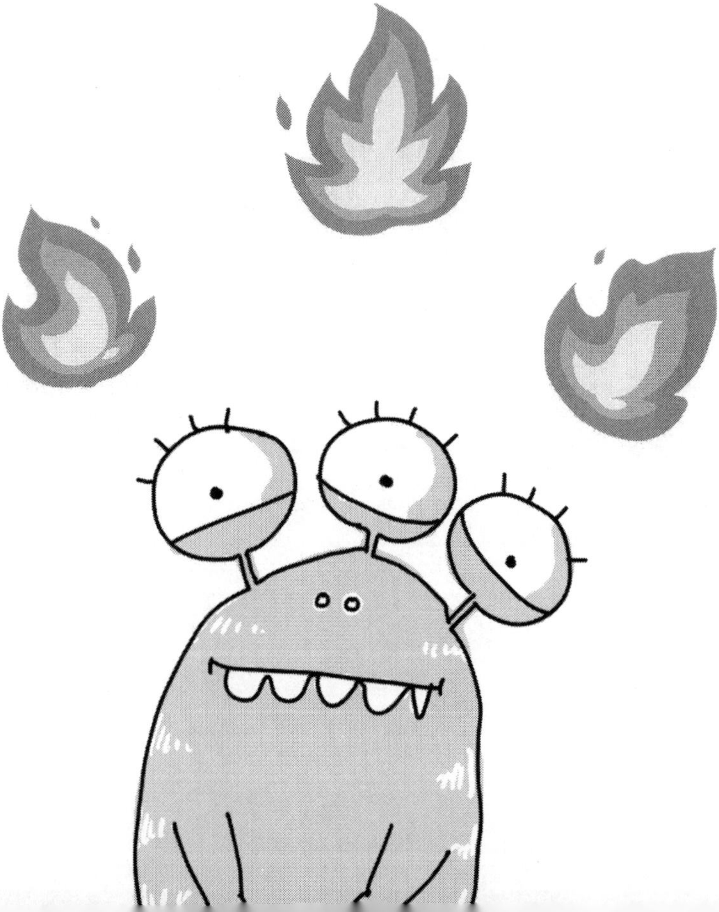

CHECK OFF ALL THE THINGS YOU COULD TRY DOING THE NEXT TIME YOU FEEL UPSET.

- [ ] **DRINK A GLASS OF WATER**
- [ ] **PAINT A PICTURE**
- [ ] **ASK FOR A HUG**
- [ ] **COLOR**
- [ ] **LISTEN TO MUSIC**
- [ ] **DANCE**
- [ ] **PLAY WITH PLAY-DOH OR CLAY**
- [ ] **COUNT BACKWARDS FROM 20**
- [ ] **SLOWLY COUNT FORWARD TO 20**
- [ ] **BLOW BUBBLES OR A PINWHEEL**
- [ ] **TAKE DEEP BREATHS**
- [ ] **TAKE A WALK OR RUN AROUND**
- [ ] **WRITE DOWN WHAT YOU ARE GRATEFUL FOR**
- [ ] **IMAGINE YOURSELF IN A CALM PLACE**
- [ ] **BAKE SOMETHING**

TELL A POSITIVE STORY BY FILLING IN THE BLANKS

IT'S A _____ DAY TODAY. THE WEATHER IS _____, THE AIR IS _____, AND I'M FEELING _____.

TODAY, I PLAN TO _____. TO DO THIS, I AM GOING TO _____, _____, AND _____.

I'D ALSO LIKE TO _____ BY _____.

I'VE BEEN THINKING OF _____ A LOT LATELY SO I'LL _____.

AFTER A LONG DAY, I KNOW I WILL NEED TO REST WHEN MY BODY _____. TO TAKE CARE OF MYSELF, I NEED TO _____. AFTER I DO THAT, I WILL FEEL _____.

THIS IS HOW I CAN MAKE IT A _____ DAY.

WHAT ARE YOUR FAVORITE THINGS BELOW?

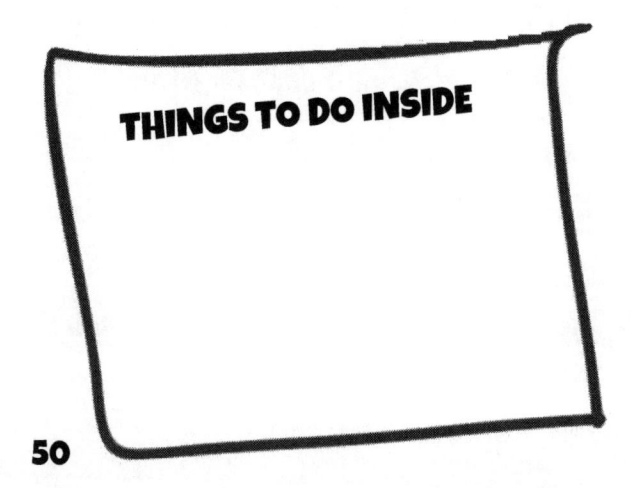

SONGS

THINGS TO DO OUTSIDE

THINGS TO DO INSIDE

HOLIDAYS

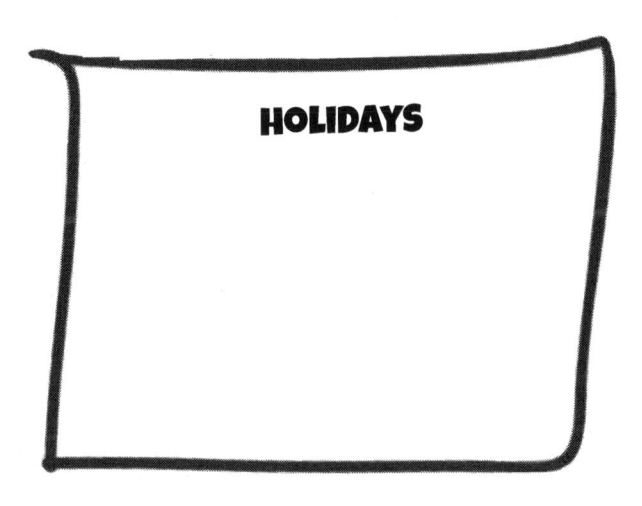

PLACES TO VISIT

THINGS TO DRAW

TIME YOURSELF FOR ONE-MINUTE AND FILL THIS PAGE WITH ALL THE THINGS THAT MAKE YOU LAUGH OR SMILE.

LOOK AROUND YOU AND WRITE DOWN ALL THE THINGS YOU ARE GRATEFUL FOR IN THESE STARS.

56

AFTER YOUR NEXT MEAL, CHOOSE ONE OF THE FOODS FROM YOUR PLATE AND SMEAR, TAPE OR GLUE A LITTLE BIT OF IT HERE.

ATTACH YOUR FOOD HERE:

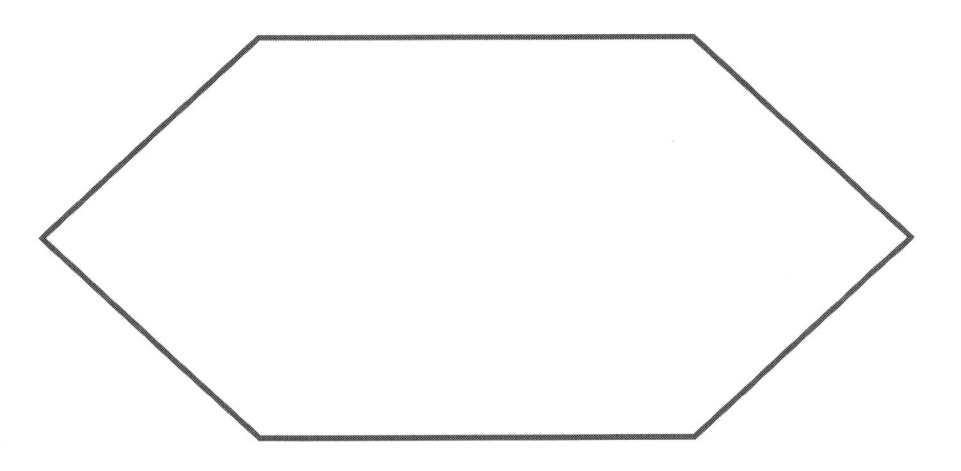

HOW DID IT TASTE?

HOW DID IT FEEL IN YOUR MOUTH?

USE A WASHABLE INK PAD OR WASHABLE MARKER TO MAKE FINGERPRINTS ON THIS PAGE.

THEN CREATE FUN PICTURES FROM YOUR FINGERPRINTS!

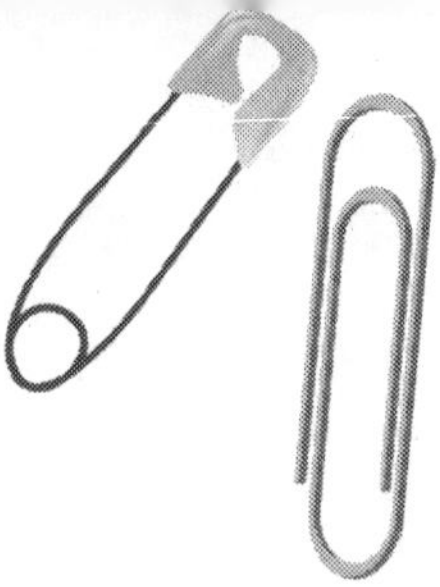
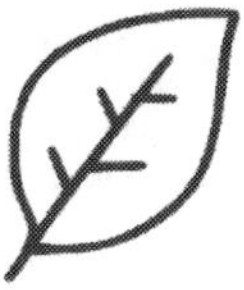
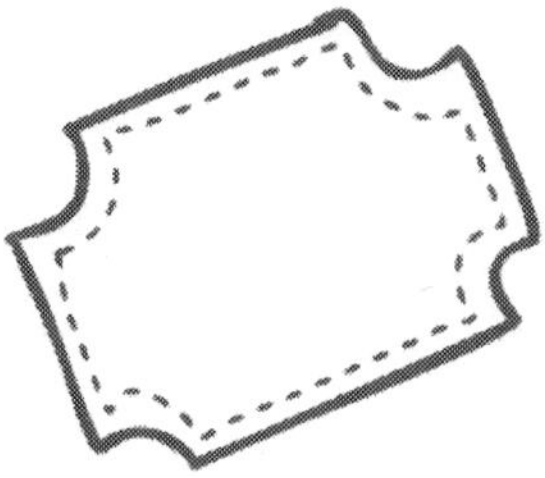
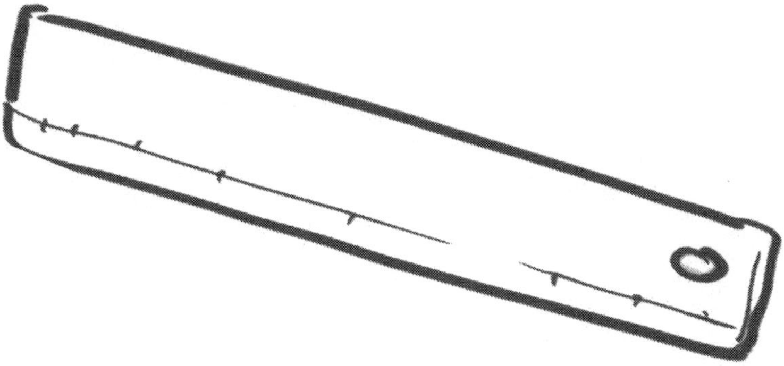
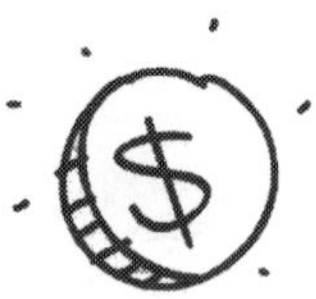
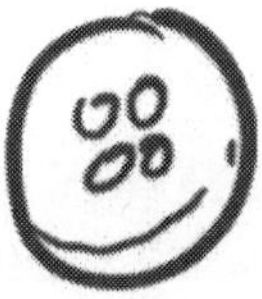

FIND A SMALL, FLAT OBJECT AND TAPE IT TO THIS PAGE.

WRITE DOWN FIVE REASONS WHY THIS OBJECT IS USEFUL.

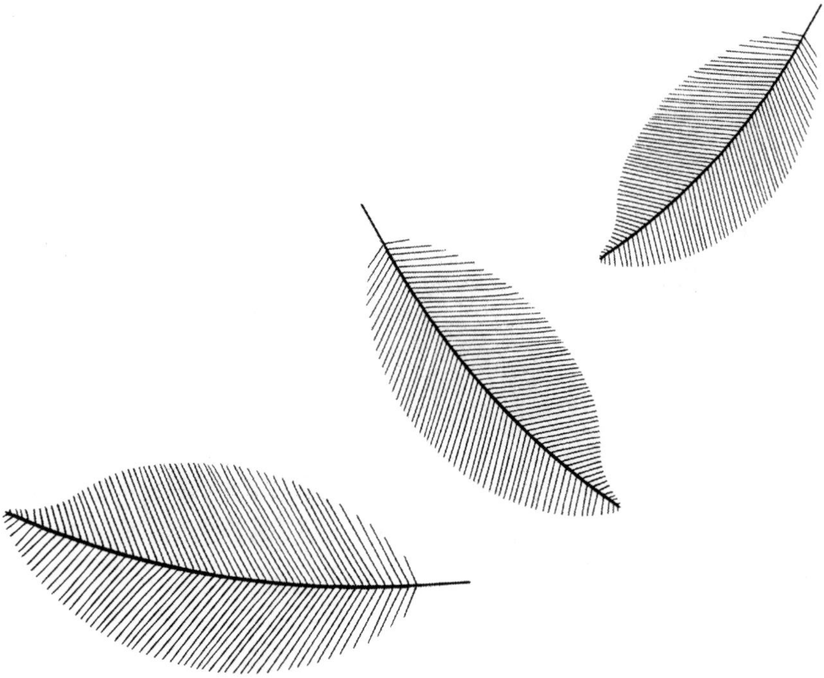

IF YOU COULD MAKE THREE WISHES TO HELP OTHER PEOPLE, WHAT WOULD YOU WISH FOR AND WHO WOULD YOU HELP?

1)

2)

3)

ASK SOMEONE TO DRAW A PICTURE OF YOU ON THIS PAGE.

NOW YOU DRAW A PICTURE OF THEM ON THIS PAGE.

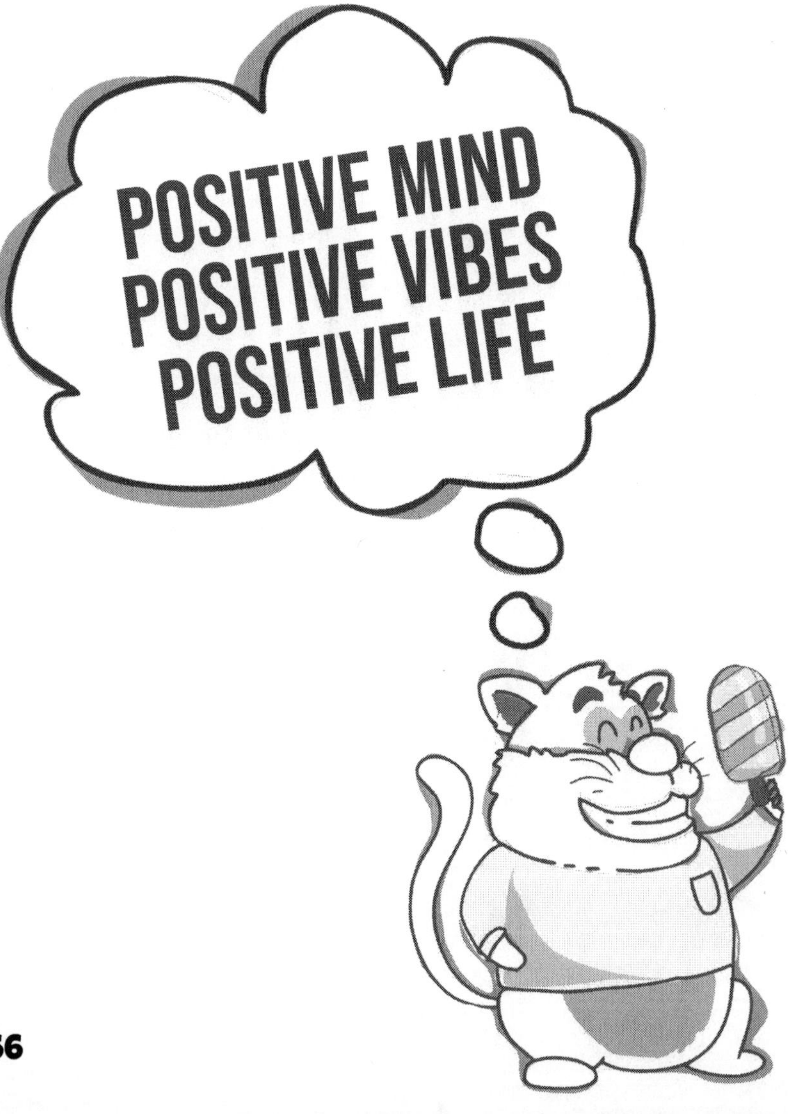
POSITIVE MIND
POSITIVE VIBES
POSITIVE LIFE

WRITE DOWN ONLY GOOD THOUGHTS AND WELL WISHES HERE.

CONNECT THE DOTS TO MAKE A PICTURE.

68

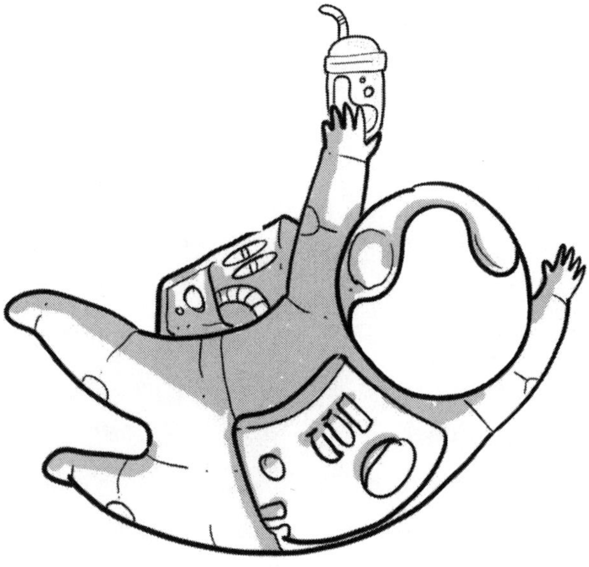

FILL THIS PAGE WITH WORDS THAT MAKE YOU HAPPY!

WHAT 7 THINGS CALM YOU DOWN?

1)

2)

3)

4)

5)

6)

7)

CAREFULLY TEAR OUT THE OPPOSITE PAGE. WRITE A KIND NOTE FOR A NEIGHBOR AND SURPRISE THEM BY LEAVING IT IN THEIR MAILBOX.

FILL THIS PAGE WITH NEGATIVE THOUGHTS, THEN CUT THIS PAGE UP AND RECYCLE YOUR NEGATIVITY AWAY.

MATCH EACH FEELING WITH WHAT YOU CAN DO WHEN YOU FEEL THIS WAY.

HAPPY	TAKE DEEP BREATHS
WORRIED	DRAW A PICTURE
CALM	TAKE A WALK OR DANCE
SAD	DRINK A GLASS OF WATER
ANGRY	ASK FOR A HUG

TIP: EACH FEELING CAN BE MATCHED TO MORE THAN ONE ACTION!

EXAMPLE:

FIND A LEAF AND GLUE IT TO THE CENTER OF THIS PAGE, THEN MAKE A DRAWING OUT OF THE LEAF.

USING A PENCIL OR MARKERS, MAKE A PICTURE OUT OF THESE PAINT DROPLETS.

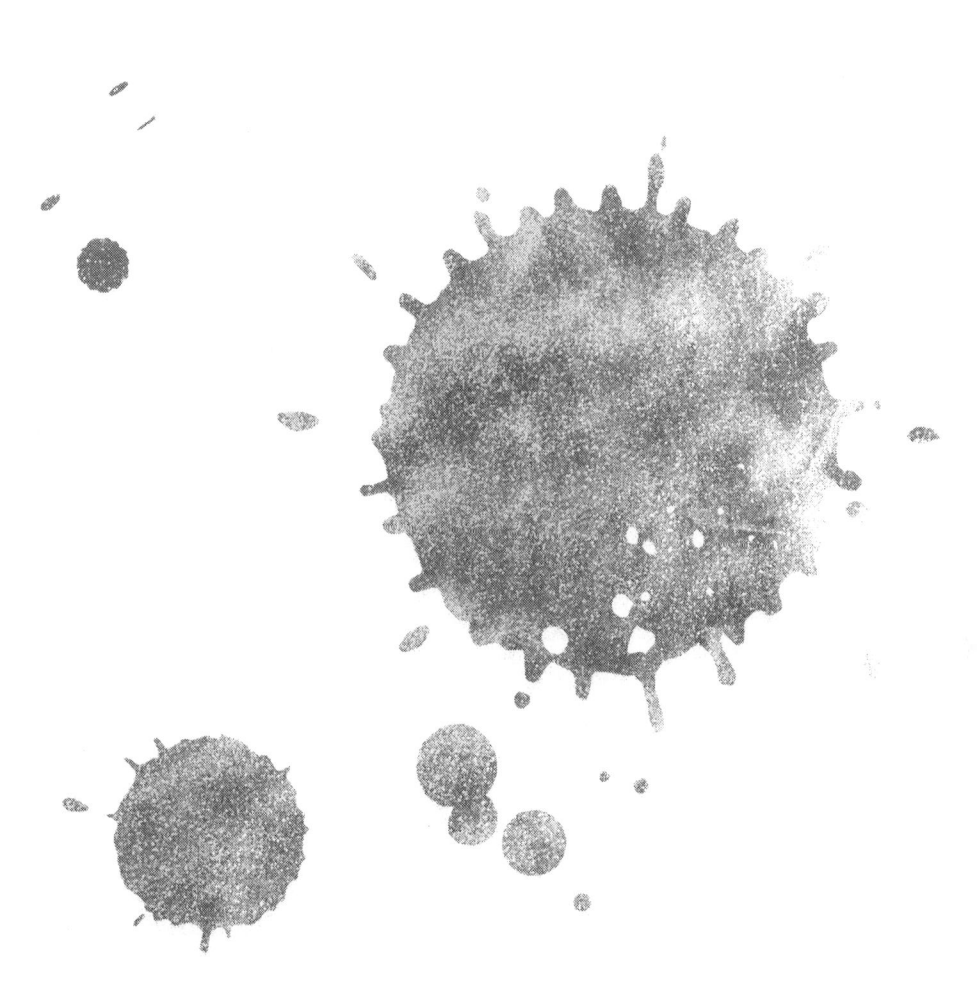

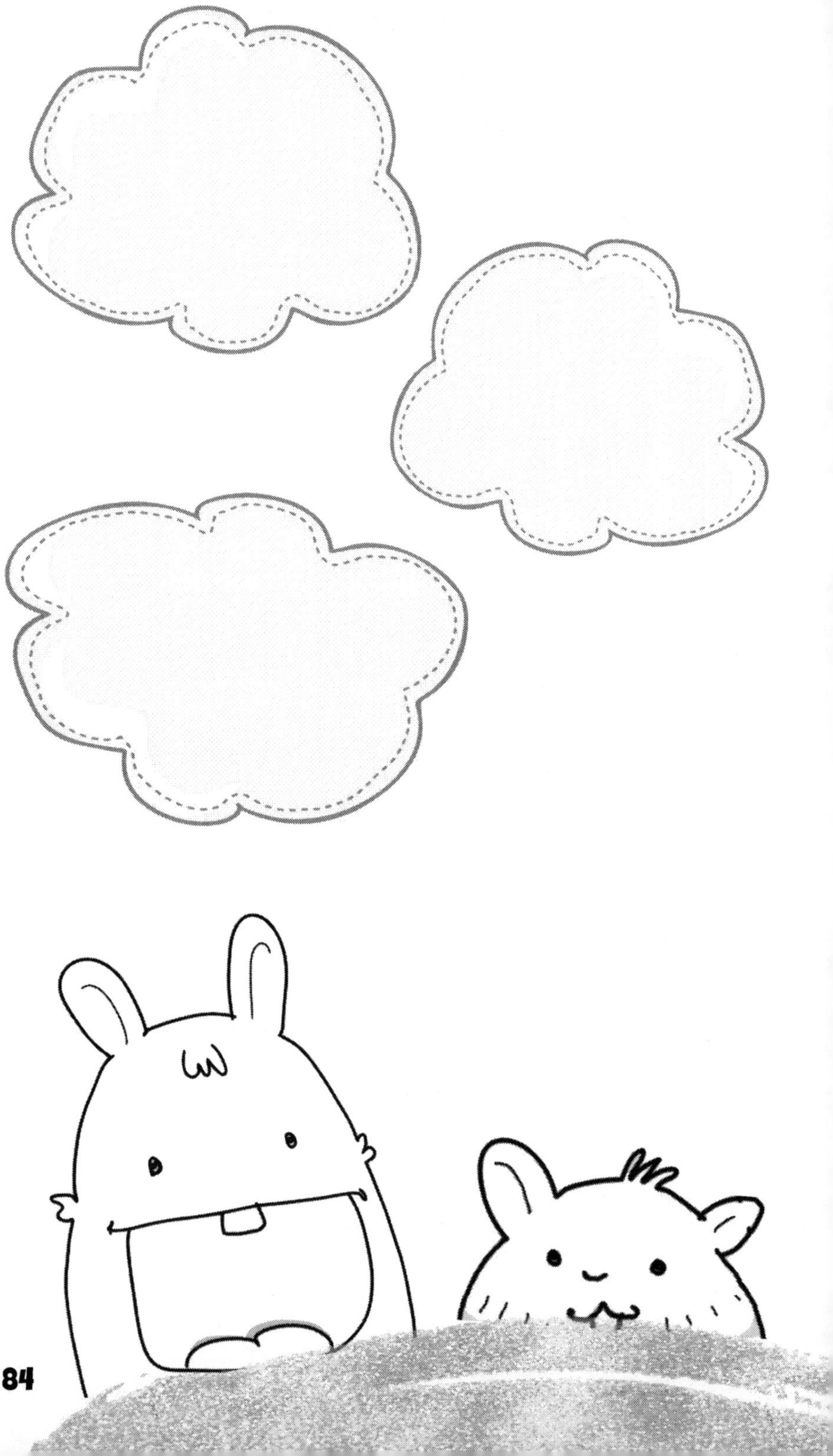

IF EACH OF YOUR FAMILY MEMBERS WERE AN ANIMAL, WHAT ANIMAL WOULD THEY BE AND WHY?

WRITE YOUR ANSWERS FOR EACH PERSON IN A CLOUD AND DON'T FORGET YOURSELF.

1 FOLD PAPER DIAGONALLY

2

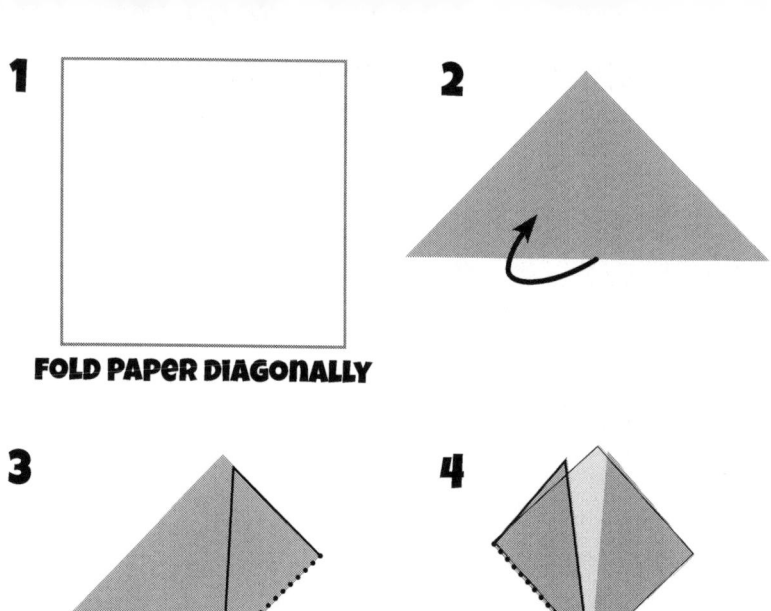

3  FOLD RIGHT CORNER UP

4 FOLD LEFT CORNER UP BRING BOTH CORNERS BACK DOWN

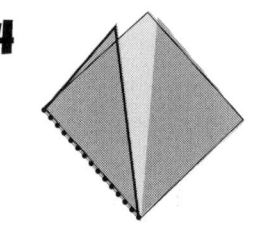

5 BEND TOP CORNER TO BOTTOM

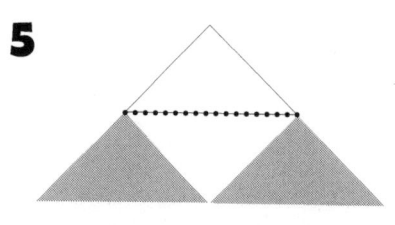

6 TUCK LEFT CORNER INTO CENTER POCKET

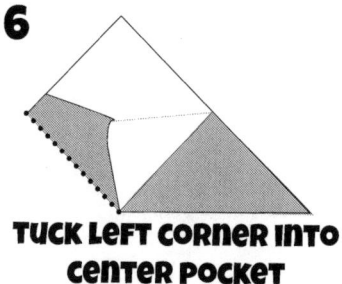

7 TUCK RIGHT CORNER INTO CENTER POCKET

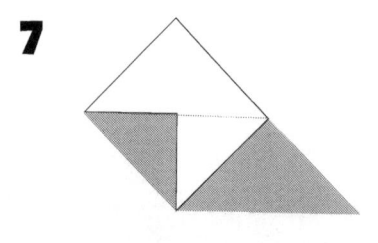

8 BOOKMARK DONE! PUT THIS OVER A BOOK CORNER

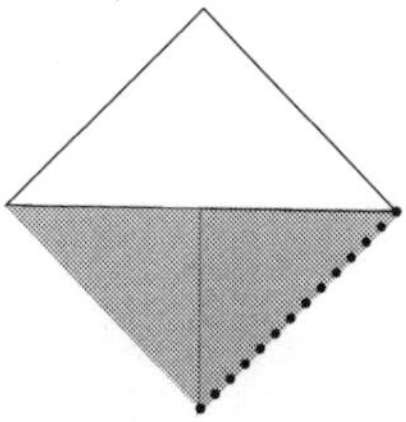

TEAR OUT THIS PAGE, THEN CUT OUT THE SQUARE BELOW TO MAKE THIS ORIGAMI BOOKMARK.

TIP: DON'T FORGET TO DECORATE YOUR BOOKMARK.

5-4-3-2-1 WORRY EXERCISE

ANY TIME YOU FEEL WORRIED, YOU CAN DO THIS EXERCISE TO FOCUS ON THE PRESENT MOMENT.

Name FIVE things you see near you.

_____
_____
_____
_____
_____

Name FOUR things you can touch near you.

_____
_____
_____
_____

Name THREE things you can hear near you.

_____
_____
_____

Name TWO things you can smell near you.

_____
_____

Name ONE food you can taste that is near you.

_____

EXTRA: A copy of this activity is at the back of this book.

EXAMPLE:

M	arvelous
A	rtistic
B	eautiful
E	xcellent
L	oving

SPELL OUT YOUR NAME IN THE BOXES BELOW. NEXT TO EACH LETTER, WRITE A POSITIVE WORD TO DESCRIBE YOURSELF.

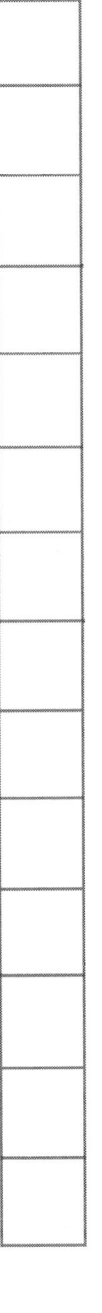

WRITE ABOUT A MISTAKE YOU ONCE MADE THAT YOU FELT BAD ABOUT.

MISTAKES HELP US LEARN AND GROW AS PEOPLE. WHAT DID YOU LEARN FROM THAT MISTAKE?

DICE GAME INSTRUCTIONS:

**PUT TOGETHER THE DICE.
START AT THE FIRST QUESTION, ROLL THE DICE AND ANSWER THE QUESTION ACCORDING TO WHAT NUMBER YOU ROLLED.**

EXAMPLE: IF YOU ROLL A ONE, GIVE ONE ANSWER. IF YOU ROLL A SIX, GIVE SIX ANSWERS.

ROLL THE DICE AGAIN AND CONTINUE TO THE NEXT QUESTION.

1) Best friends

2) Favorite games

3) Sports you enjoy playing or watching

4) Favorite animals

5) Favorite colors

6) Favorite movies or television shows

7) Yummy fruits or vegetables

8) Favorite desserts

9) Things that smell good

10) Things that make you feel happy

**CAREFULLY TEAR THIS PAGE OUT.
CUT OUT THIS OPENED DICE AND FOLD ON THE LINES,
THEN GLUE OR TAPE THE TABS TO MAKE A CUBE.**

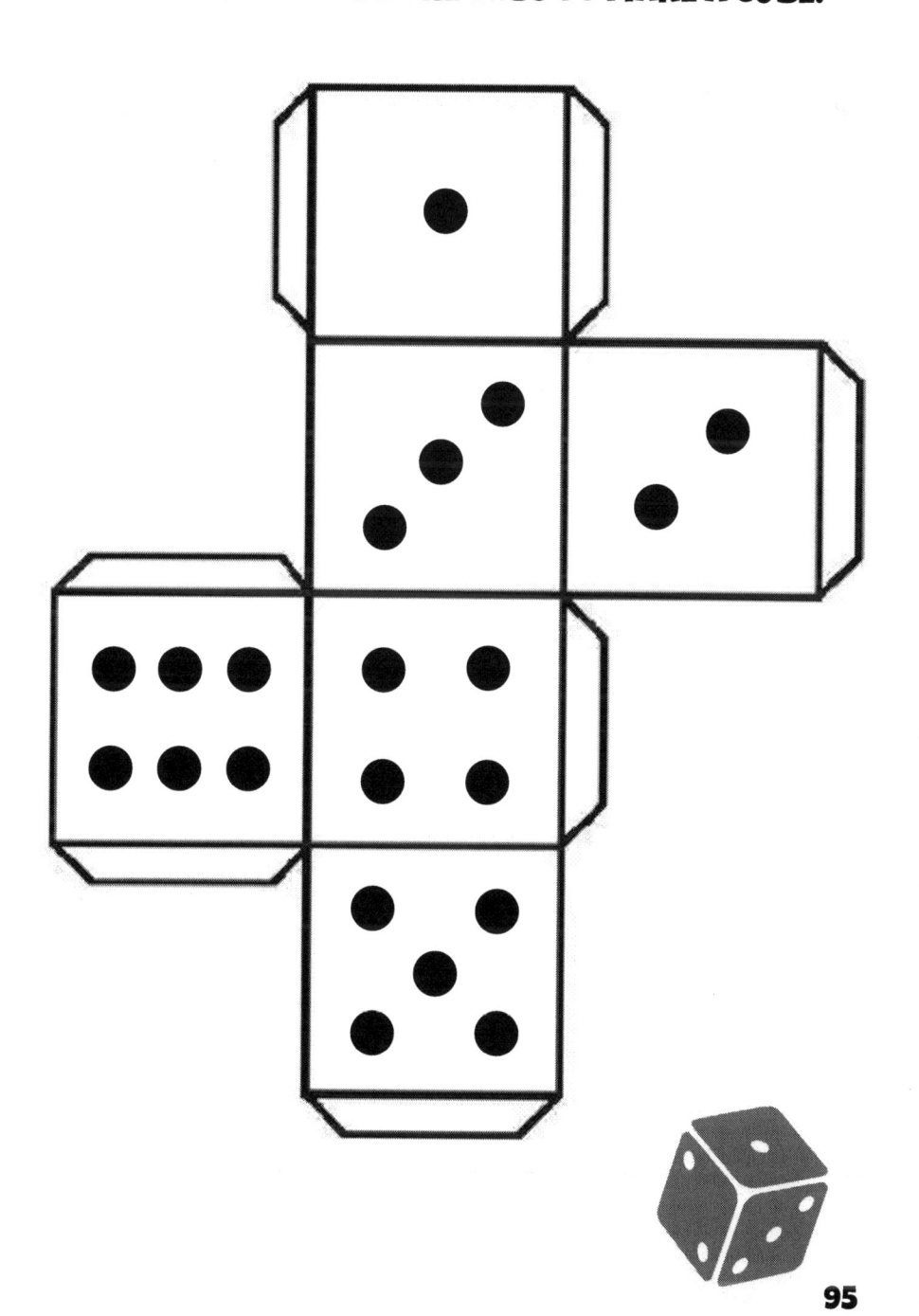

95

DRAW PICTURES OF THREE THINGS YOU WOULD LIKE TO LEARN.

WRITE DOWN YOUR FAVORITE JOKES HERE.

DONUT WORRY, BE HAPPY!

TELL YOUR FAVORITE KNOCK KNOCK JOKE.

KNOCK KNOCK

WHO'S THERE?

WHO?

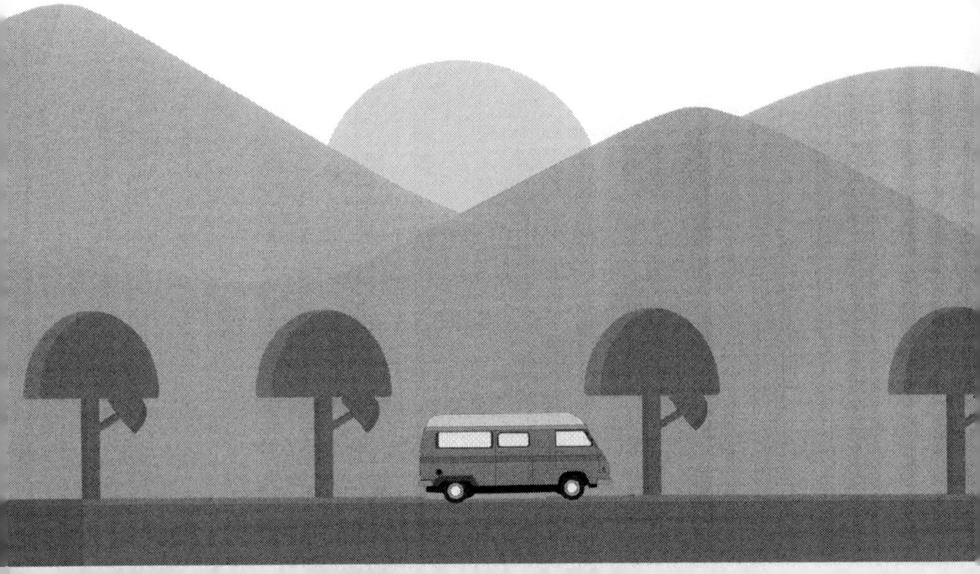

IF YOU COULD GO ON VACATION SOMEWHERE...

WHERE WOULD YOU GO?

WHO WOULD YOU INVITE TO JOIN YOU?

WHAT WOULD YOU PACK?

WHAT WOULD YOU LIKE TO DO THERE?

WHAT'S THE BEST THING YOU'VE EVER...

SEEN?

TOUCHED?

HEARD?

SMELLED?

TASTED?

YOU

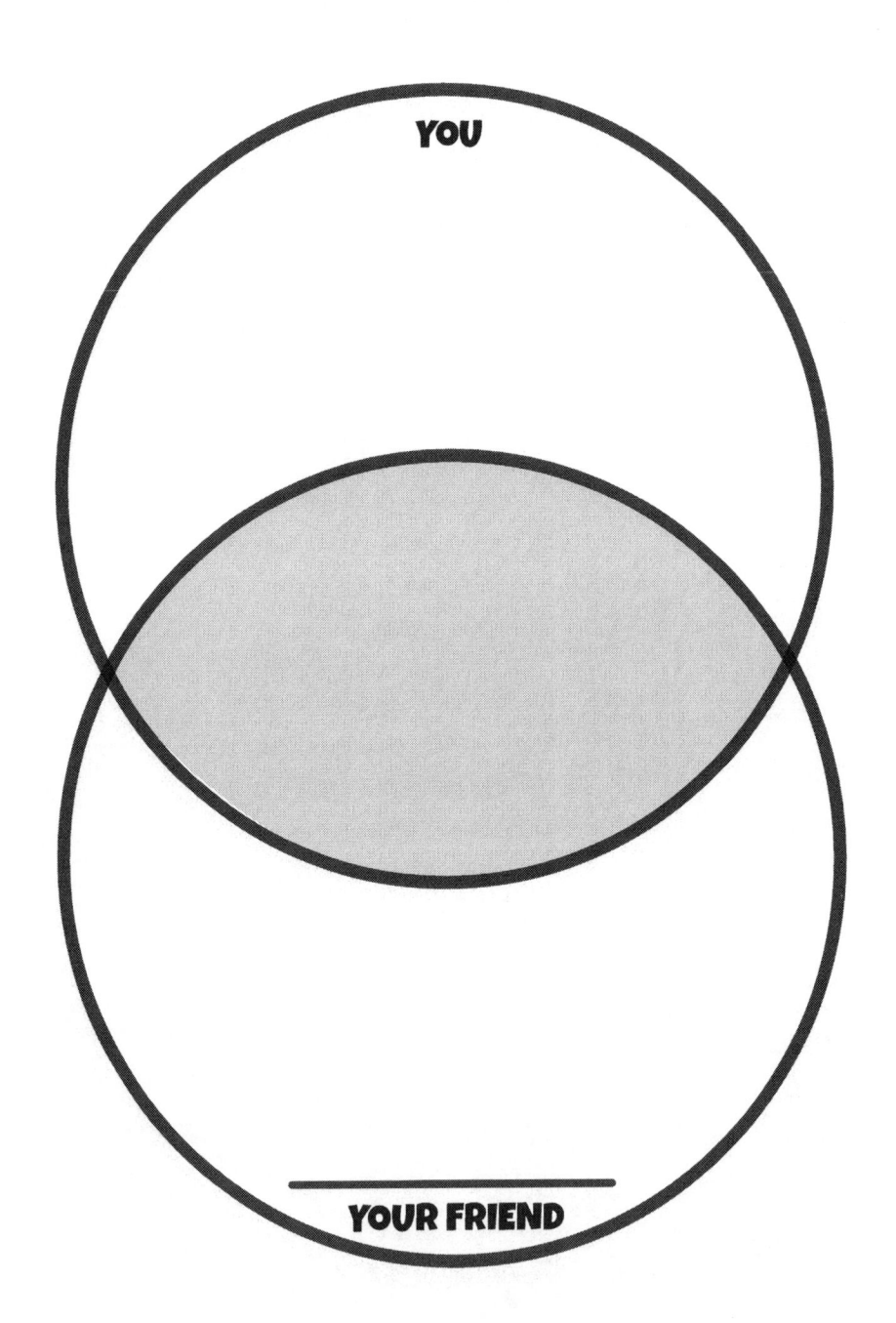

YOUR FRIEND

FRIENDS

1) FILL IN THE TOP CIRCLE WITH THINGS THAT MAKE YOU SPECIAL AND DIFFERENT.

2) WRITE THE NAME OF A GOOD FRIEND AND FILL IN THE BOTTOM CIRCLE WITH THINGS THAT MAKE THAT PERSON SPECIAL AND DIFFERENT TO YOU.

3) IN THE SHADED OVERLAPPING PART OF THE TWO CIRCLES, WRITE WHAT YOU AND YOUR FRIEND HAVE IN COMMON.

COMPLETE THESE SENTENCES.

My word of the week is _____

The best part of my day is usually when I

I feel sad when _____

When I am frustrated, I _____

Taking deep breaths help me _____

I focus on being positive by _____

EXAMPLE:

Dear Pencil,

You are my best friend. When I wake up in the morning and get ready for school, I make sure we are together.

Thank you for helping me share the ideas in my head and get them onto paper. I also love that you have an eraser so I can keep improving what I write down. You're just amazing!

Love,
Me

THINK OF AN OBJECT YOU USE EVERYDAY.

WRITE A LETTER TO THIS OBJECT TELLING IT HOW MUCH YOU APPRECIATE IT.

POWER POSING IS A WAY OF STANDING TO MAKE YOU FEEL STRONGER OR MORE CONFIDENT WHEN YOU DON'T FEEL YOU CAN DO SOMETHING.

WHENEVER YOU WANT A BOOST OF COURAGE, STAND LIKE THIS FOR 2-MINUTES.

MAKE SURE YOU STAND TALL WITH YOUR SHOULDERS BACK, CHEST OPEN AND HANDS ON YOUR HIPS WHILE LOOKING FORWARD.

TRY THIS POWER POSE A FEW TIMES, THEN WRITE DOWN HOW YOU FELT AFTER.

WRITE DOWN WHAT MAKES YOU AMAZING ON THESE STICKY NOTES.

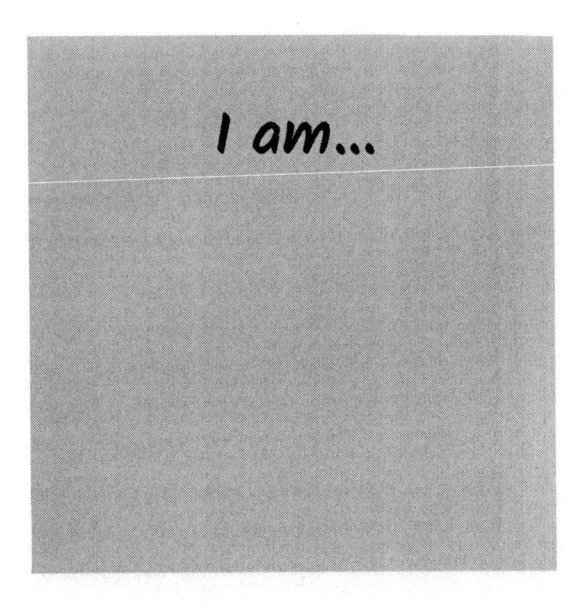

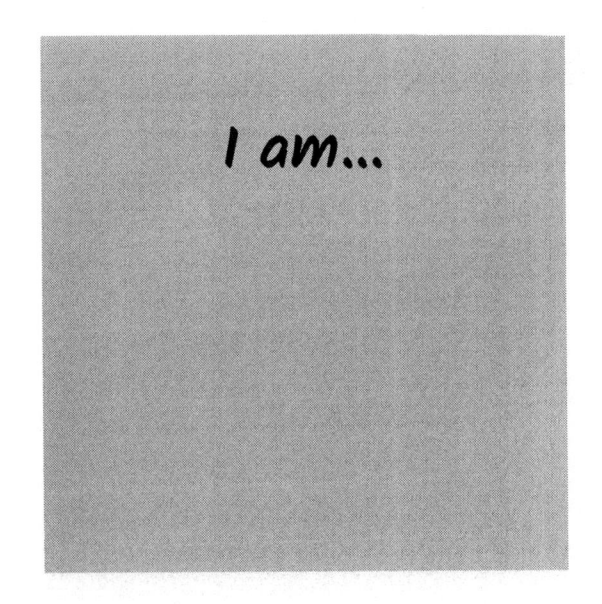

I am...

I am...

I am...

I am...

LET'S PRACTICE MINDFUL LISTENING

THE NEXT TIME SOMEONE TALKS TO YOU, TRY HAVING A MINDFUL CONVERSATION BY:

1. LISTENING WITH YOUR FULL ATTENTION.

2. MAKING EYE CONTACT WITH THE PERSON TALKING.

3. WAITING UNTIL THE PERSON FINISHES TALKING BEFORE SAYING SOMETHING BACK.

AFTER YOU TRY THIS, WRITE YOUR OBSERVATIONS HERE.

Did you feel different when you focused on having a mindful conversation? If so, how?

Do you think the person could tell you were giving them your full attention? How could you tell?

Are there any other things you noticed?

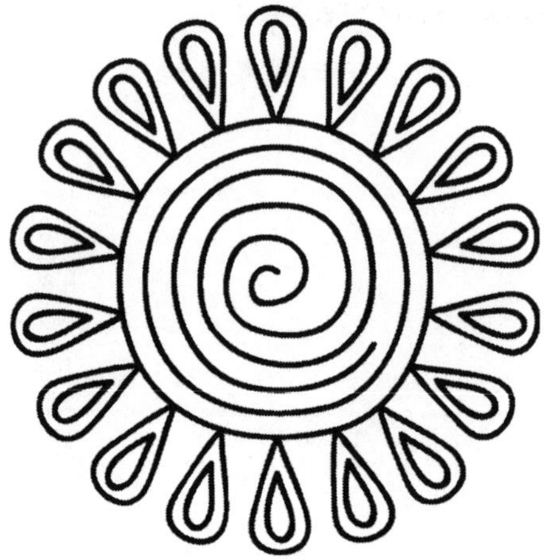

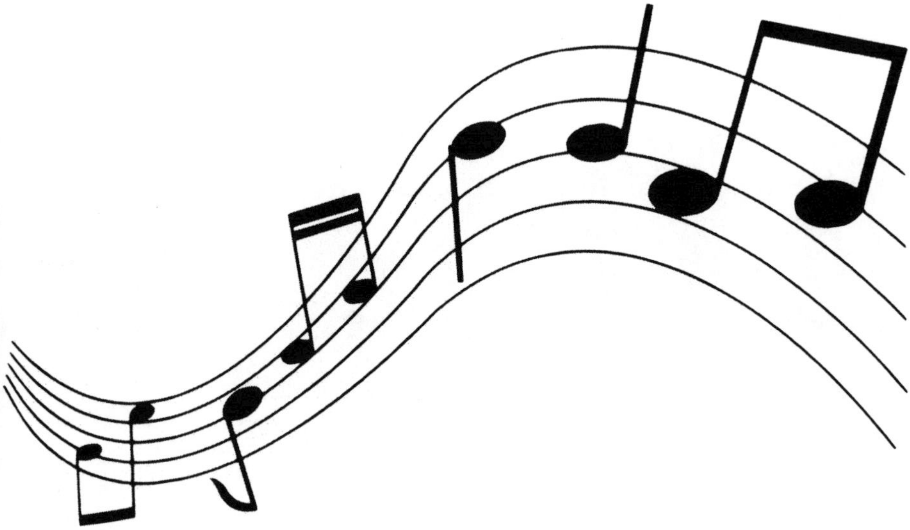

PLAY SOME CALMING MUSIC AND COLOR THESE PAGES.

IF THERE WAS A BOOK WRITTEN ABOUT YOU, WHAT WOULD BE ON THE FRONT COVER?

WHAT WOULD IT SAY ON THE BACK COVER?

FILL THIS PAGE WITH THINGS YOU LIKE.

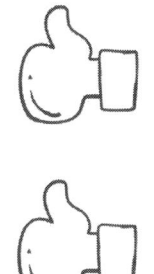

BELIEVE

CHOICE

GRATEFUL

HAPPY

KINDNESS

MINDFUL

LIVE

LOVE

POSITIVE

THANKS

POSITIVITY WORD SEARCH

```
M I N D F U L C E S
A K D D D O I O D P
C I D D V D V M D O
H N D E D D E P U S
O D B E L I E V E I
I N B V D O E S D T
C E T H A N K S D I
E S D D A D D I D V
U S D R Y P P A H E
N D G R A T E F U L
```

CLOUD MEDITATION

FIND A QUIET PLACE TO RELAX AND LAY DOWN OUTSIDE.

SPEND 5-10 MINUTES OBSERVING THE CLOUDS IN THE SKY.

Tip: If you start to think of something else, just gently remind yourself to focus back on the clouds in the sky.

WHAT SHAPES DID YOU SEE?

WHAT COLOR WAS THE SKY?

WHAT ELSE DID YOU NOTICE?

DID YOU THINK OF OTHER THINGS WHILE YOU DID THIS MEDITATION?

HOW DID YOU FEEL AFTER THE MEDITATION?

USING YOUR LESS DOMINANT HAND, DRAW A PICTURE OF SOMETHING YOU ARE GRATEFUL FOR.

FOR EXAMPLE: IF YOU ARE RIGHT-HANDED, USE YOUR LEFT HAND TO DRAW AND IF YOU ARE LEFT-HANDED, USE YOUR RIGHT HAND TO DRAW.

USING YOUR TOES TO HOLD A PENCIL OR PEN, DRAW A PICTURE OF SOMETHING YOU ARE GRATEFUL FOR.

NOW SHOW BOTH OF THESE PAGES TO SOMEONE AND SEE IF THEY CAN GUESS WHAT YOU DREW.

TURN THESE TWO PAGES INTO A GRATITUDE WALL.

DECORATE THEM WITH THINGS YOU APPRECIATE IN YOUR LIFE.

**IDEAS: YOU CAN DRAW PICTURES, COLOR, STICK THINGS HERE OR WRITE WORDS THAT GIVE YOU STRENGTH.
BE CREATIVE!**

SOLVE THE EXAMPLE MESSAGE BELOW, THEN CREATE A KIND MESSAGE FROM THE KEY DECODER. GENTLY TEAR THE PAGE OUT AND LEAVE IT SOMEWHERE FOR SOMEONE TO FIND AND SOLVE.

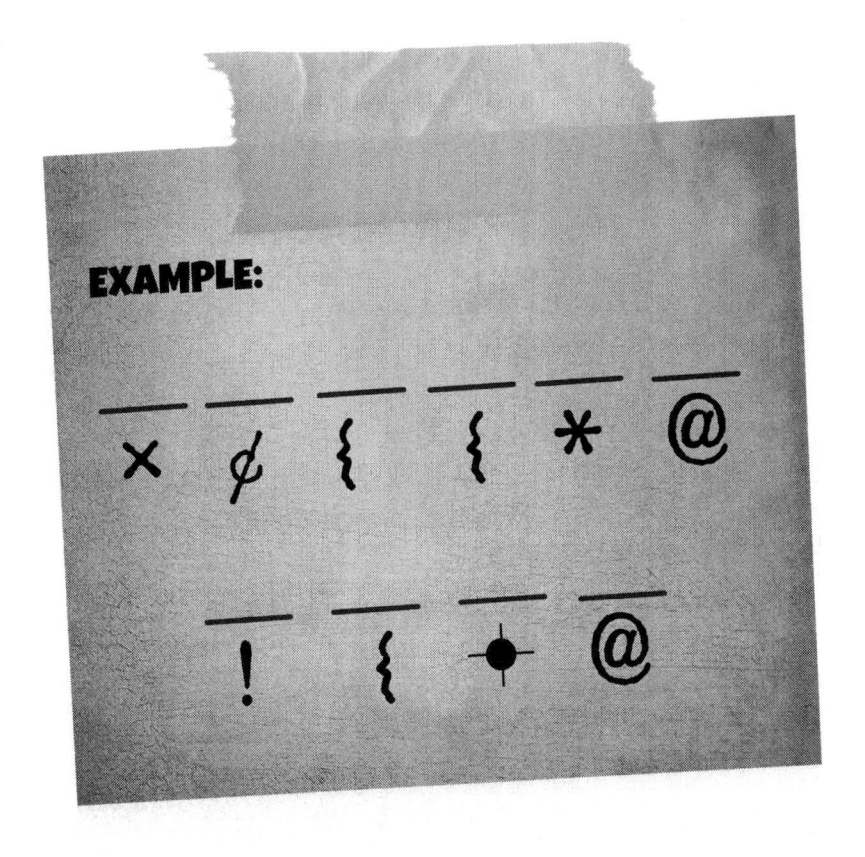

EXAMPLE:

___ ___ ___ ___ ___ ___
 ×   ¢   {   {   *   @

___ ___ ___ ___
 !   {   •   @

130 *EXTRA: A copy of this activity is at the back of this book.*

A	B	C	D	E	F	G	H	I	J
#	<	×	:	@	®	>	¢	÷	+
K	L	M	N	O	P	Q	R	S	T
=	!	$	¥	{	~	"	©	*	;
U	V	W	X	Y	Z				
£	✦	X̄	>	&	•				

IF YOU WERE AN ADULT, WHAT RULES WOULD YOU CHANGE FOR KIDS?

WRITE DOWN TEN 4-LETTER THINGS IN THE ROOM.

1)

2)

3)

4)

5)

6)

7)

8)

9)

10)

WRITE A SHORT MESSAGE TO THANK EACH OF THESE PEOPLE HERE.

Postal Carrier

Healthcare Worker

CAREFULLY TEAR OUT THESE PAGES, CUT OUT THE NOTES OUT AND DELIVER THEM.

Teacher

Grocery Store Worker

FIND A FLOWER THAT HAS ALREADY DROPPED TO THE GROUND AND FLATTEN IT IN THIS BOOK.

WRITE ALL THE BEAUTIFUL THINGS YOU IMAGINED THIS FLOWER EXPERIENCED DURING ITS LIFE.

CIRCLE 11 WAYS YOU CAN TAKE CARE OF YOUR MIND.

Meditate or do yoga

Exercise

Play video games all day

Practice gratitude

Read a book, paint, draw or color

Watch a lot of news

Spend time outside

Blaming yourself when you make a mistake

Do acts of kindness

Focus on positivity

Remember all problems are temporary

Be around people who make you happy

Listen to your favorite music

Remember that mistakes are chances to learn and grow

Be around people who make you feel sad

CIRCLE 11 WAYS YOU CAN TAKE CARE OF YOUR BODY.

Meditate or do yoga

Eat lots of candy and ice-cream

Exercise or play sports

Eat lots of fruits and vegetables

Stay awake late

Drink plenty of water

Brush your teeth at least twice a day

Play outside as much as possible

Get enough sleep

Shower once a month only when your body stinks

Take a shower or bathe regularly

Wash hands often

Relax and watch movies on the couch all day

Find a friend you can go walking with

Practice breathing exercises

142 EXTRA: *A copy of this activity is at the back of this book.*

THINGS TO DO

**WRITE A LIST OF THINGS YOU WANT TO DO
IN BETWEEN THE DOTTED LINES, THEN
CUT ON THE DOTTED LINES AND LEAVE THEM ATTACHED.**

**ONLY TEAR EACH PAPER OUT
AFTER YOU HAVE FINISH DOING EACH TASK.**

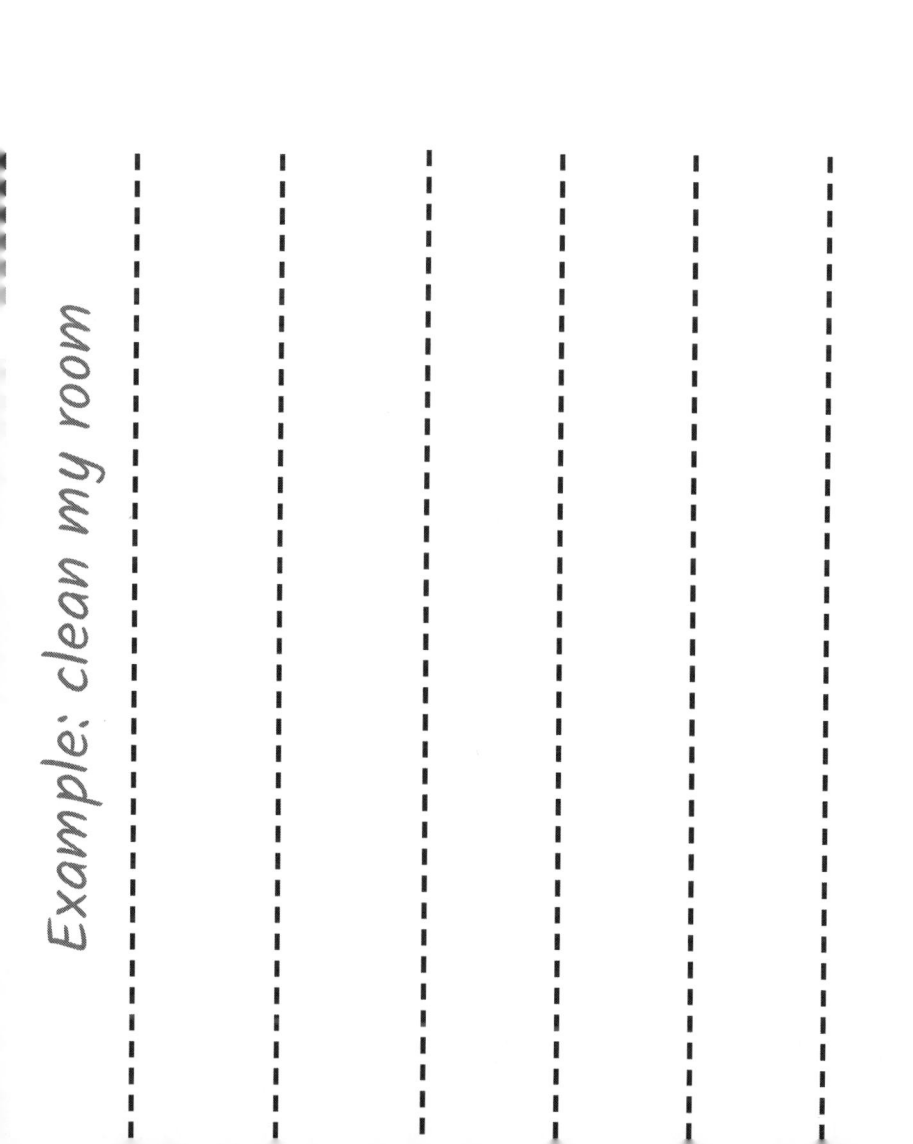

Example: clean my room

WHAT AMAZING THINGS ARE HAPPENING THIS WEEK?

DRAW A PICTURE OR WRITE ABOUT IT.

CHANGING NEGATIVE THOUGHTS

ON THIS PAGE, WRITE DOWN SOME OF YOUR NEGATIVE THOUGHTS.

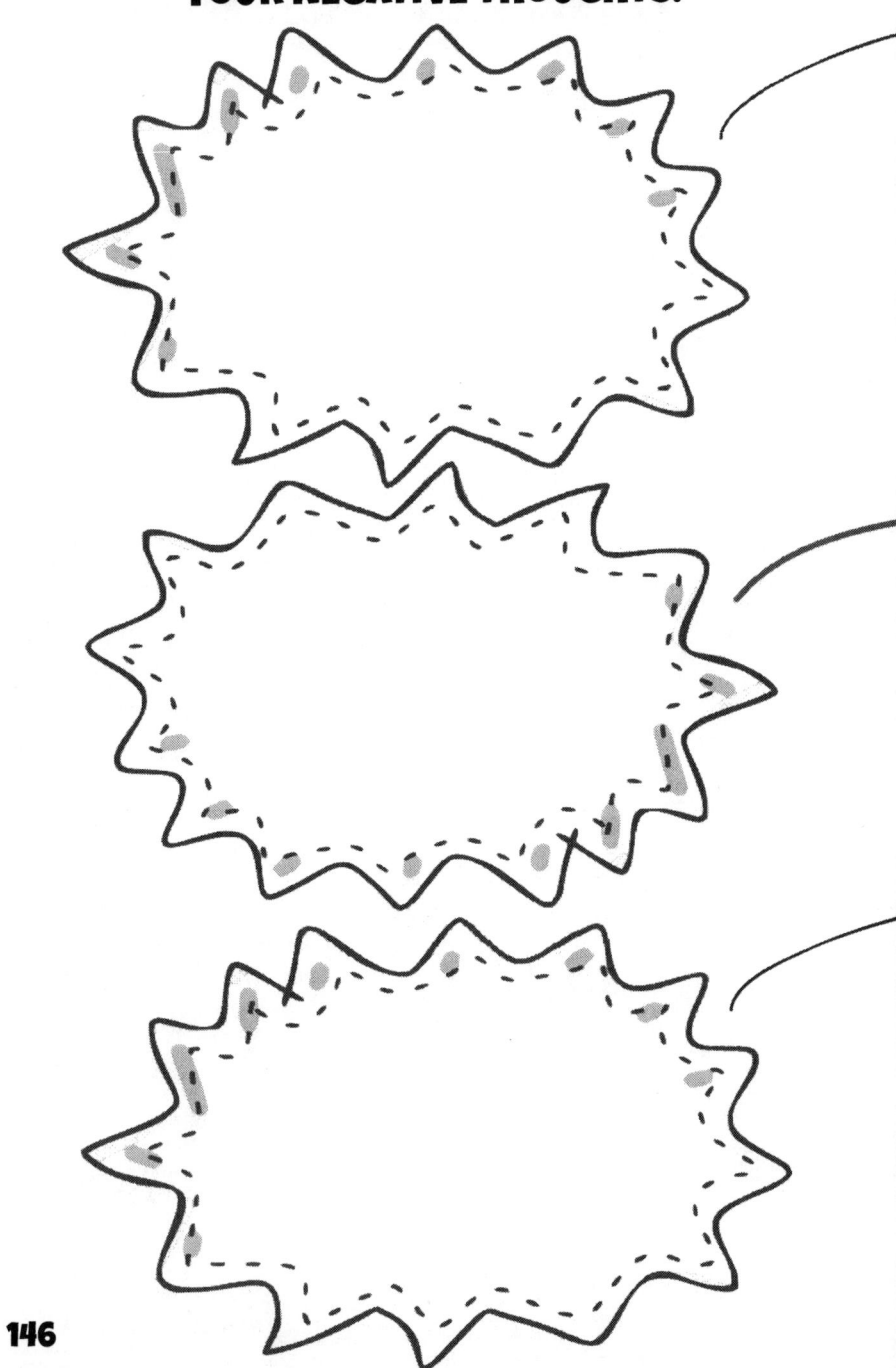

ON THIS PAGE, THINK OF HOW YOU CAN CHANGE THAT NEGATIVE THOUGHT INTO A POSITIVE ONE.

147

148

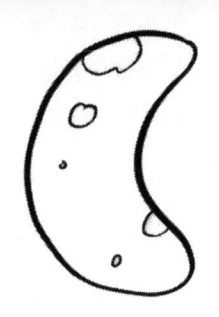

BODY RELAXING EXERCISE

TIGHTEN THEN RELAX EACH BODY PART TWICE, THEN CHECK IT OFF BELOW.

HOW DO YOU FEEL AFTER?

- [ ] HEAD
- [ ] FACE
- [ ] SHOULDERS
- [ ] HANDS
- [ ] ARMS
- [ ] STOMACH
- [ ] BACK
- [ ] BOTTOM
- [ ] LEGS
- [ ] TOES

COME BACK TO THIS PAGE ANYTIME YOU FEEL YOU NEED TO RELAX YOUR BODY AGAIN.

TRY THE YOGA TREE POSE

THE TREE POSE HELPS YOUR BALANCE AND FOCUS.

IT ALSO MAKES YOUR BACK, STOMACH, AND SHOULDERS BECOME STRONGER.

SEE IF YOU CAN STAND LIKE THIS FOR 10-20 SECONDS.

Put your hands together over your head

Stand up tall and look straight ahead

Press your standing foot into the ground as if your foot is a tree's roots. Put the other foot on your leg above the knee and balance!

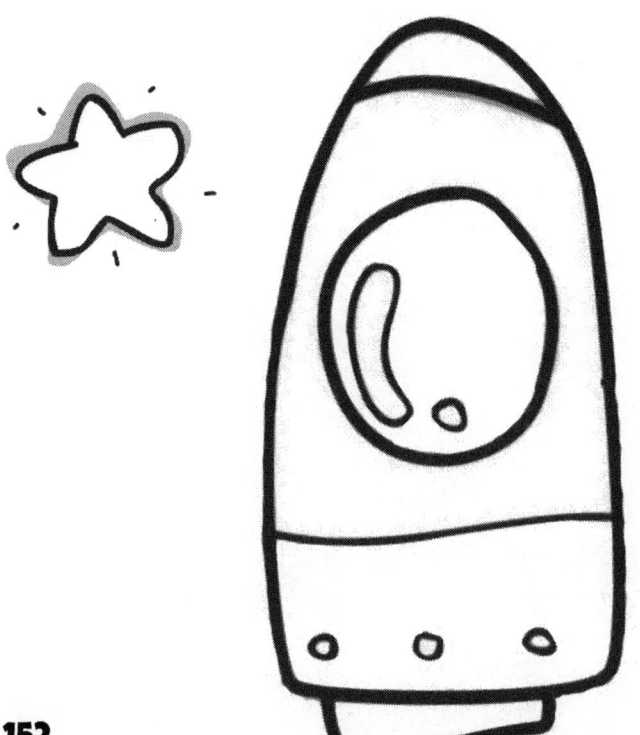

TIME CAPSULE

**WRITE 10 THINGS YOU ARE GRATEFUL FOR
THAT YOU CAN PUT INTO THIS
TIME CAPSULE TO BE OPENED 100 YEARS FROM NOW.**

1)

2)

3)

4)

5)

6)

7)

8)

9)

10)

EXTRAS

DRAW A PICTURE IN THIS BOX, THEN CAREFULLY TEAR OUT THE PAGE. CUT OUT THE PUZZLE ON THE BACK AND PIECE IT BACK TOGETHER AGAIN.

Cut out the puzzle on the dotted lines.

DRAW A PICTURE IN THIS BOX, THEN CAREFULLY TEAR OUT THE PAGE. CUT OUT THE PUZZLE ON THE BACK AND PIECE IT BACK TOGETHER AGAIN.

Cut out the puzzle on the dotted lines.

FILL YOUR BUCKET WITH THINGS PEOPLE CAN DO FOR YOU OR SAY TO YOU TO BRIGHTEN YOUR DAY?

YOU CAN ALSO FILL A BUCKET FOR SOMEONE ELSE.

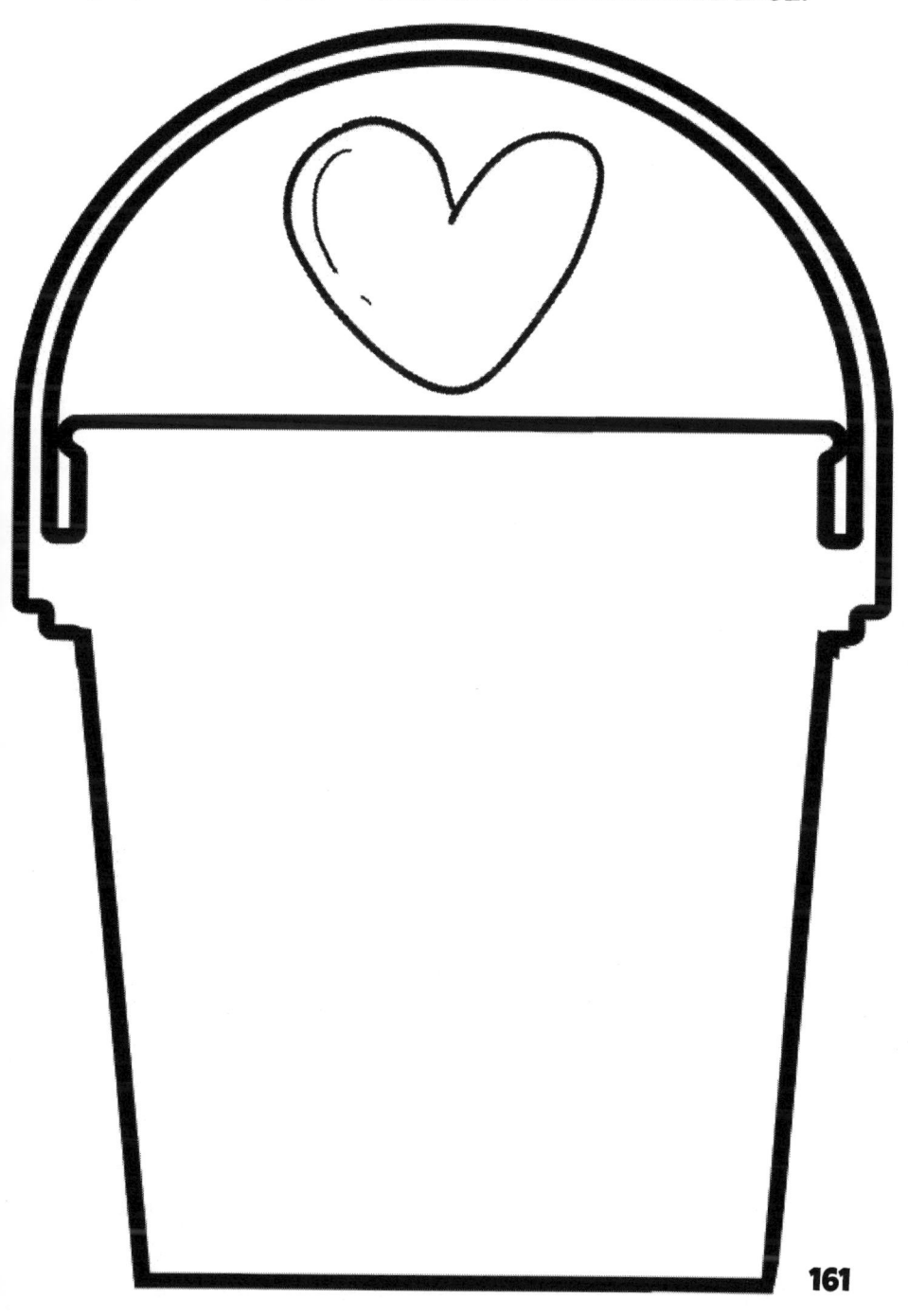

SIGN POSTS CHALLENGE

**THINK OF AN OBJECT
THAT YOU MIGHT SEE EVERDAY.
EVERY TIME YOU SEE THIS OBJECT TODAY,
WRITE DOWN SOMETHING YOU ARE GRATEFUL FOR.**

OBJECT EXAMPLE: A BALL, A PAINTING, OR A PLANT...

5-4-3-2-1 WORRY EXERCISE

ANY TIME YOU FEEL WORRIED, YOU CAN DO THIS EXERCISE TO FOCUS ON THE PRESENT MOMENT.

Name FIVE things you see near you.

_____
_____
_____
_____
_____

Name FOUR things you can touch near you.

_____
_____
_____
_____

Name THREE things you can hear near you.

_____
_____
_____

Name TWO things you can smell near you.

_____
_____

Name ONE food you can taste that is near you.

_____

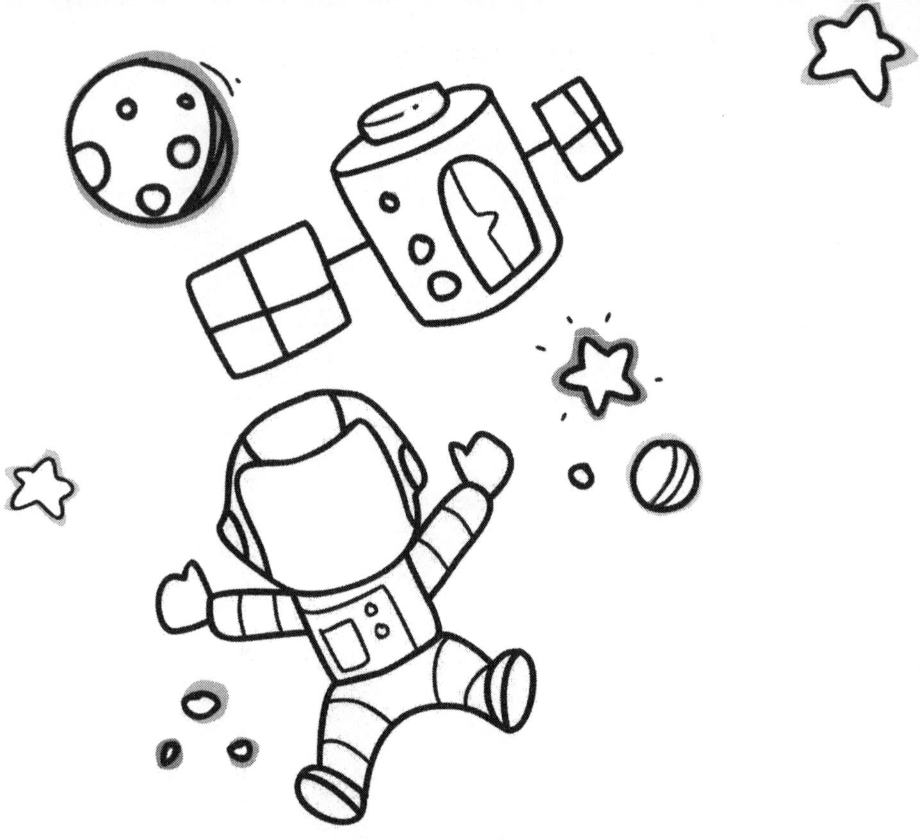

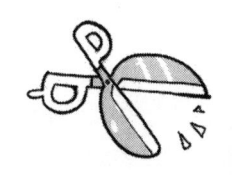

THINGS TO DO

WRITE A LIST OF THINGS YOU WANT TO DO IN BETWEEN THE DOTTED LINES, THEN CUT ON THE DOTTED LINES AND LEAVE THEM ATTACHED.

ONLY TEAR EACH PAPER OUT AFTER YOU HAVE FINISH DOING EACH TASK.

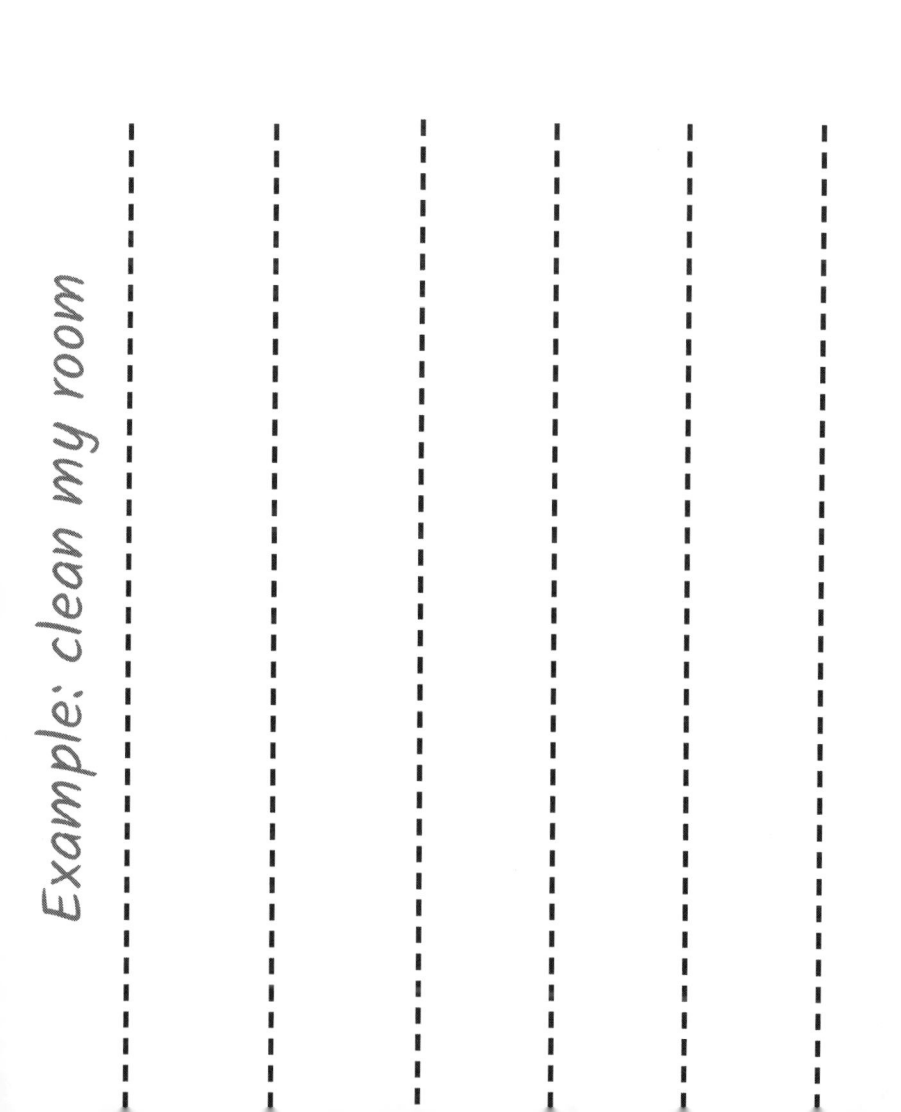

Example: clean my room

A	B	C	D	E	F	G	H	I	J
#	<	×	:	@	®	>	¢	÷	+
K	L	M	N	O	P	Q	R	S	T
=	!	$	¥	{	~	"	©	*	;
U	V	W	X	Y	Z				
£	✦	X̄	>	&	•				

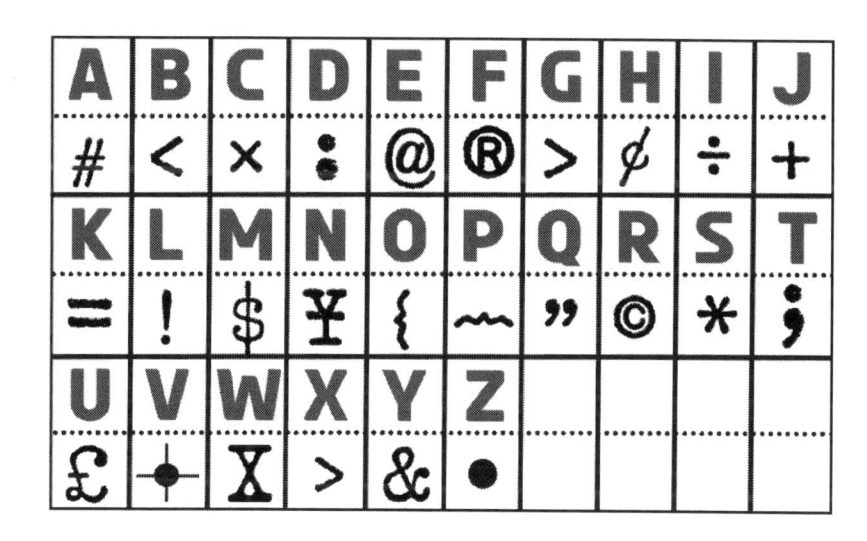

ON SEPARATE SHEETS OF PAPER, CREATE TWO POSITIVE MESSAGES FROM THE KEY DECODER. GENTLY TEAR THIS PAGE OUT, CUT ALONG THE DOTTED LINES AND DELIVER YOUR TWO MESSAGES AND A DECODER TO TWO PEOPLE TO SOLVE YOUR MESSAGE.

A	B	C	D	E	F	G	H	I	J
#	<	×	:	@	®	>	¢	÷	+
K	L	M	N	O	P	Q	R	S	T
=	!	$	¥	{	~	"	©	*	;
U	V	W	X	Y	Z				
£	✦	X̄	>	&	•				

NOTES

NOTES

DRAWING SPACE

NOTES

DRAWING SPACE

NOTES

DRAWING SPACE

NOTES

DRAWING SPACE

**FOR ALEXI AND ARIE,
MY CREATIVE ASTRONAUTS**

YOU ARE AWESOME!

Made in the USA
Monee, IL
12 May 2022